D0645389

Sea of Miracles

∞

An invitation from the angels

∞

Deepening your *every day, everywhere*
connection to the messengers of the Divine

Sea *of* Miracles

an invitation from the angels

Amy Oscar

She has a special gift !

E-SPIRITED MEDIA, A DIVISION OF AS IF, LTD.   NEW YORK

Copyright c 2011 by Amy Oscar

All rights reserved. No part of this book may be reproduced or transmitted in any form or by any means, electronic or mechanical, including photocopying, recording, or by any information storage and retrieval system, without permission in writing from the author.

Permissions: amy@amyoscar.com

Published by E-Spirited Media, a division of As if, Ltd.

Printed in the U.S.A.

Design by Julie Schwartz, Wyndjammr Consulting & Design

Library of Congress Cataloguing-in-Publication Data

Oscar, Amy
Sea of Miracles: an invitation from the angels-2nd ed
1. Spirituality 2. Angels I. Title

ISBN 978-1461036852

10 9 8 7 6 5 4 3 2 1
Second edition

What you seek is seeking you.

Rumi

To light, love, life.

Sea of Miracles
Contents

Introduction

Years ago, before everyone had a cell phone, I ran out of gas on the Throgs Neck Bridge, a massive span of steel suspended over the Long Island Sound, 12 miles from New York City. As my car lost all its power, the steering wheel locked and we rolled to a stop in the right lane, just after the curve. From this position, oncoming motorists couldn't see us until they were 50 feet away. Approaching at 60 mph, they swerved around us, brakes screeching. Several shouted rude remarks, shaking their fists.

I could make excuses: It was Thanksgiving and we were running late. I had a terrible cold. My two-year-old daughter had been screaming on and off for two hours, upsetting her four-year-old brother and distracting me. Exhausted, overwhelmed, I'd missed the red fuel light on my dashboard. Still, it hardly mattered *why* we were stuck—I had to do something to protect my children, and my car, from being hit from behind.

My son was fast asleep. Pulling my wailing daughter from her car seat, I set her on my hip and walked behind the car. There, I began flapping my free arm like a broken windmill, warning approaching motorists away.

In the high November winds, with a guardrail only up to my thigh, Katie and I could easily have been blown right off the bridge!

God help us! I shuddered.

Instantly, a small red fire truck pulled behind my car, lights flashing. At the exact same moment, a Boar's Head truck pulled in front of us. *Provisions,* read the sign, painted on its side. We were saved!

"I almost hit you," said the driver of the fire truck. "I was looking down changing the radio stations and wham! There you were! Walking down the road with this baby in your arms. What a picture!"

As he went to search for the bridge's emergency phone, the other driver spoke to me quietly. "Ran out of gas?" he asked. "Happened to me once."

"Really?" I asked. I felt instantly better, calmer and a good deal less ridiculous. He told me to wait in the car for the tow truck, which he explained, would push my car off the bridge. "Get off at the Clearview and pull over first chance you get. I'll drive ahead and get you some gas."

"Bless you, thank you," I said.

The tow driver arrived, barking instructions. He would push my car from behind. "Put it in neutral, stay off the brakes," and BANG! we were off. He pushed, I steered, doing some of the deep breathing I'd been saving for emergencies, and we made our bumpy, jerky way down the exit ramp. I pulled into a grassy embankment at the side of the highway and stopped to wait for the Boar's Head driver to deliver the gas.

But "You idiot!!!" the tow truck driver came running from behind. "You had an angel meeting you, you didn't listen."

"What? I don't..."

"That guy, he was meeting you at the Clearview, *the Clearview*," he shouted, face red. "This is the Cross Island!" Then, storming back to his truck, he left us there.

I cried for a while. Then, I got out of the car. I put a blanket around Max's shoulders and wrapped Katie inside my jacket. We began to walk toward some stores that I could see behind the embankment. If I can find a deli, I thought, I can get something warm for the children to eat. We could go to the bathroom. Maybe they'll let me use the phone...

We'd gone only a few yards when...

"Mommy," Max asked. "Who's that man by our car?" I turned and there he was—the driver of the Boar's Head truck, already putting gas in our car.

When I tell this story, I usually leave out the part where he lifted one end of my car and shook it, to make the gas run into the lines. It seems so outlandish that even I'm unsure sometimes if that really happened. I skip ahead to the part when my car was turned on, the engine humming, the heat warming my children's hands and I turned to thank our rescuer.

"Let me pay you for the gas," I said, holding up a twenty, all the money I had. "Let me buy you dinner."

He smiled, and I noticed, for the first time, his beautiful eyes. "You keep it, Ma'am," he said. "You go home and live a good life and raise these kids. That will be thanks enough for me."

"But," I stuttered. "I want to do something… at least, tell me your boss's name, I'll send a letter."

"My boss knows how sweet I am," he said, smiling. "Go on home."

As he walked away, I scribbled down the name of his company and the phone number painted on the side of his truck. Then, I put my car into gear and drove my children to their grandparents' house. All the way there, I composed the letter in my head. I imagined the gift I'd send: an American Express gift certificate, tickets to a show…

But a few days later, when I called the number that I'd carefully copied into my journal, it was out of service. When I phoned the Boar's Head company they told me there was no distributor in the town that had been painted on the side of that truck, nor was there one on record with its name.

Back then I didn't know how to explain it. But I do now: he was an incarnated angel, sent, in a truck marked *Provisions,* to rescue two children and a frazzled mom from the top of a bridge, and to remind us: *You are never alone.*

Today, I am here to say the same thing to you.

For the past six years, since 2004, I've been reading stories about angels — stories from real people from around the world who've had direct, personal encounters with the Divine: people just like you.

I've read stories of terminal illnesses that were instantly healed; disembodied voices shouting life-saving commands; mysterious nurses who appear beside hospital beds in the middle of the night to offer comfort; doctors who materialize at accident scenes to speak life saving advice before emergency crews arrive and then disappear without a trace.

I've read stories about lost heirloom jewelry — watches, wedding rings, diamonds — suddenly found. I've read about children led home by gentle strangers no one's seen before (or since); flocks of butterflies returning day after day to comfort the grieving; birds that visit the lonely, the frightened, the seriously ill — bringing the courage and hope they need to survive.

I have always believed in angels, people often begin or, *I've never been sure about angels… but I am now!*

I knew just what they meant. Though I'd worked with spiritual materials for 25 years, as a spiritual counselor, writer, and teacher, though I'd experienced many things that couldn't be explained as mere coincidence I simply wasn't prepared for the way that reading those stories would change my life.

You see, I didn't believe in angels. To me, the winged and haloed messengers were the stuff of myth — they were metaphors, I thought, an attempt for human beings to explain their interactions with something they couldn't quantify, see or understand any other way.

I believed in that *something* — and I'd built a relationship with the presence that seemed to be everywhere, always available to listen to my prayers or read over my shoulder as I scribbled in my journal.

Little did I know—a well-worn phrase, beloved by storytellers and editors that perfectly sums up my state of mind when this project began. For little did I know, as I opened the first letter and began to read, that these stories would deliver—drop by precious drop—an infusion of Grace straight to my heart.

Little did I know that this work was a response, sent to answer my most fervent prayer, *Please fill my life. Give me something meaningful to do. And please, oh, please make it about more than just me.*

That's the thing about miracles, they rarely come as we expect them to. There's no flutter of wings, no dramatic flash of lightning. Most miracles come gently, subtly, in a slow-moving wave of Grace only discernible when it's over.

This is the story of how I was transformed from Editor to Witness, from Student to Teacher, and from being a person who wrote about other people's lives to a person living fully at the center of my own.

This book is an invitation—and a guidebook. For after six years of swimming in this miracle sea, I can honestly say: angels are everywhere, every minute of every day—and all you have to do to bring them into your life is open the door, and welcome them in.

Sea of Miracles

I.

Encountering Angels

–

You are not alone

The angels showed me:
You are not alone. We are here. We are with you, as we have always been, every day, everywhere.

Encountering Angels

When I was a teenager, I had a powerful dream that I've never forgotten. I dreamt that I was falling, dropping through vast empty space like a stone. The earth rushed toward me at breathtaking speed and terrified, I braced for impact, pulling my body into a tight knot of fear. But I didn't hit the ground.

Instead, I slowed down—floating like a feather on a cushion of warm wind. I landed gently on a soft surface—the upturned palm of God.

I've got you, I heard, the words whispered clearly, close enough that I could feel, on my ear as I woke up, the breath of the messenger. *I've got you:* a message I've been receiving in countless ways, ever since.

ONE

You Are Not Alone

Patterns in Angel Stories
Opening to the presence of the Divine

If you've read books like this one before, you've read the statistics: polls have been taken, percentages tallied. It's clear that most people—60, 70, 80 percent—believe in angels. Angels are mentioned in the texts of Judaism, Islam and Christianity and people all over the world enter houses of worship each week to read stories in which angels play a part.

And yet, one of the first things I noticed when I began reading angel stories was the defensive, almost argumentative tone so many writers were taking: *This is my angel experience,* they wrote. *It really happened.* Many wrote, *No one will believe me.* In a world that seems both obsessed with faith—and with testing the faith of others—I wasn't all that surprised. It's weird to go around talking about this stuff—weirder still to claim to have proof.

Still, I was intrigued that even after having been ridiculed, discounted and disbelieved, people seemed compelled to try again. *I've told this story again and again. Maybe this time someone will believe me.*

I could detect no pattern in the kind of person who wrote in. Believers, non-believers—and people of all faiths (including agnostics and atheists) were experiencing miracles—and these were only the ones who were reporting their stories! How many others were out there?

Miraculous encounters were being reported by people who never attended religious services; and by people who showed up every week. Some people wrote, *I don't really believe in God* or, *I don't go to church very often*. Still, others wrote: *I have always believed ...*

There seemed to be no pattern in the kinds of people reporting angelic encounters. In fact, the only real pattern I could discern was the pattern in the encounters themselves.

- **Calling out (Asking):** In every story, before an angelic encounter, *someone had called out for help.* Sometimes, a formal prayer was said. Just as often — more often, in fact — the person had simply pleaded: *God help me!* Even when a writer didn't include this detail in their account, when I called someone and asked, "Did you pray or ask for help?" They always said, "Of course!"

- **A Calming Presence:** Almost every writer reported the presence of a calming, peaceful energy; one woman described it as being swept with a broom of light. Encounters with this presence stabilized the emotions, wiping away fear, doubt, panic and confusion, even in the most harrowing situations. *I just knew things would be okay,* they reported.

- **Intuitive flashes and/or imagery:** Angelic encounters were often accompanied by intuitive feeling impressions. People experienced vivid mental images or somehow knew what to do or to say.

- **Visible 'light':** Very few people *saw* anything. Those who did reported seeing balls of light or 'orbs' (some even captured the light balls in photographs). People saw <u>outlines of light</u> or <u>glowing clouds of light</u> in dark corners—even in daylight. In a few stories, people saw and interacted with <u>beings who</u>, they wrote, *seemed to be made of foggy white light.'*

- **No wings, no haloes:** There were stories about angels in flowing white robes and some people saw wings. But almost every time, these visions were experienced while sleeping, in dreams. Yet there were thousands of <u>accounts of *embodied angels:* mysterious strangers who appear in human form</u>, looking just like you or me, do something to help and then withdraw, disappearing without a trace!

- **Sound:** Some people heard a particular sound when angels were present, often a high-frequency "crickets chirping" or "bees buzzing" sound. This sound, which I experience myself, differs from the ringing ears of tinnitus: it isn't always present; and, astonishingly I could ask the angels to turn it down to a more comfortable volume (and they did!)

- **Unusual/out-of-the-ordinary events:** A book falls from a shelf, open to a meaningful page; a dream image appears in waking life; a stranger wearing out-of-place clothing delivers a life-altering message; a bird flies into your windshield. The list of bizarre things that could happen seemed infinite. For every person, the <u>angels seemed capable of literally coordinating the universe to deliver a personally meaningful sign.</u>

And then there were the voices.

Some <u>people heard their own names, whispered</u> in an ear, often as they awoke from a dream—a kind of punctuation mark that told them, *Wake up and take note of this message.* Others heard <u>voices</u> that

coming up *mt are* *mt are*

warned them, in specific, detailed language, away from treacherous situations—on mountainsides, highways, at the edges of oceans and swimming holes. Parents were firmly told, *Move the baby now!* preventing a precious child from being struck by a rogue wave, a drunk driver—even a wild horse!

People received clearly spoken driving instructions: *Hit the brakes now!* or *Get in the right lane!* Even my friend Susan told me she'd heard a voice once, while driving. *Slow down—now!* it commanded. She hit the brakes instantly, avoiding a high-speed rear end collision with a car that cut in front of her seconds later. It was only after she was safe and the crisis averted that she thought to ask: Where did that voice come from?

Still unconvinced these phenomena were really *angels,* I searched for an explanation in psychology and neuroscience. Perhaps these "voices" were some sort of coping mechanism, I thought, a projection of our own psyche—like an inner automatic pilot that, combined with a flood of adrenaline (which focuses us) and endorphins (which calm us) might make people believe they are having a supernatural experience.

NO!

That would have been impressive enough. But it didn't explain how someone else—often a child, would ask, "Who was speaking?" or "Mommy, who was that man who told you what to do?" It didn't explain either, how the voices seemed to know what was going to happen in the future.

I began to notice that these stories had a lit up, almost electric quality.

The stories activated a particular kind of 'listening' in me, like an inner alertness that was switched on as I read. Later, when I spoke with the people who'd sent the stories, who'd personally experienced a Divine encounter, they described the same kind of energy—that calming sense of certainty. "I had no doubt that what I experienced was real," they told me. "It was the simplest message but it changed everything." "My life," they told me, "has never been the same."

I kept reading.

I began to sort the stories into categories: Highway Angels, Hospital Angels, Rescue Angels, Angels at the beach. It was a natural thing to do—the stories did seem to fall into distinct groups.

Months passed, then a year, two years, then three. As I continued to read more stories, a strange new energy coursed through my body—it was like absorbing or swallowing light! After work, I'd carry that energy to the grocery store or an evening class. I felt lighter—and people began to respond to me in a different way. They'd smile more and engage me in conversation.

Once, at a writer's conference where I was a panelist, a woman sat down opposite me to ask a question. I expected a polite query about an article submission or story idea. When she asked, "Have you seen an angel?" I was so surprised that I stammered out an inelegant, "W-w-w-hat?"

There was no way she could have known about the work I was doing. My name was not associated with the stories then and the conference organizers had listed me only as "Editor."

"I'm sorry," she shook her head. "I don't know what made me ask that. I…" she took a breath. "Wait, yes I do know. It's your face. It looks lit from underneath the skin. I'm…well, I'm able to see angel light. It's something I can do—and I can tell that you've seen angels."

When I told her about my work, she said, "I thought so. I can always tell."

∞

A Waterfall of Grace

There were other signs that my life was being touched—and graced—by the presence of angels. Opportunities fell into my lap; doors opened; money showed up when I needed it and I developed an uncanny knack for finding parking spots at the mall!

Everything that had happened to me before was given a new context. Things I'd written off as strange but inexplicable phenomena began to form a pattern that made my own life look more guided, which made me feel, you know, kinda special…

That didn't last. As the angels showed me: *You are all special, all guided. These things are happening to everyone, every day.*

I experienced a profound shift in the way that I see (and the way that I live) as all of these stories—along with the spiritual teachings I'd studied for years—began to weave themselves into a braid of wisdom that I'm still unraveling, a spiraling gift of meaning. One day, I knew: *I can no longer pretend that what I'm experiencing isn't real.*

I began to detect the presence of an alternate path, running parallel to the path that I was on.

Glowing and apart, I saw that this path was an invitation to an alternate way of thinking and living that could be accessed at any time, at any age, by anyone. Though the path came to me as a dream-like image, it was also completely and palpably real. I saw that it had always been there, beckoning me to fully experience what I'd been dabbling in for years: a deeper and more meaningful relationship with the Divine.

And here I must come clean—for even though this is a book about angels—and even though every story I read came to me under the banner of 'angel stories,' it soon became clear to me that, running like a stream beneath every story and every encounter of my own, there was another Divine presence. It was less articulated than the angels—bigger, wider, deeper—but it was just as responsive. I sensed that the angels were but one expression, one part of this vast and loving 'something more.'

Through this avalanche of angel stories, I began to understand: I am witnessing the presence of the Divine—of *God*. As this realization dawned, so did an increasing sense of responsibility to report it—to tell *you* about it. Like the letter writers who seemed compelled to share their stories, even when others had doubted them, I, too, felt the urge to bear witness. "If I touch just one person," I thought (and I continue to think) then I've done my job. This compulsion, I've come to understand, is the natural response to gratitude.

I won't lie to you. I was terrified.

I made all kinds of excuses. I got sick, got busy with other things and got caught up in family dramas. But each day, because of the nature of my work, I was called back to reading miracle stories. Reading them, I was called back to closer relationship with the Divine—and an ever-increasing proximity to that glowing path, that *invitation*.

I knew that accepting this invitation would require me to live in a new way: Heart open, eyes clear, feet firmly planted on the ground as the whole living world dissolved into shimmering mystery. This is the story of what happened when I did just that—and what can also happen for you.

Grace Note: **Presence**

In the Old Testament story, when Isaac was called by God, he answered, "Hineni." Translated from the Hebrew, *hineni* means, "Here I am, for you called me."

In the Bible, the word hineni is used when God personally calls on someone to do something difficult and important. "Here I am," Abraham responds to God's call; "Here I am," replies Moses. It's such a simple statement and yet, it's one of the most powerful things a human being can say. Here I am: ready, willing and able.

Ready, Willing and Able

This is how angels show up in our lives: ready, willing and able to help. Here I am, they tell us, through signs and synchronicity. Here I am, for you called me.

When they show up, we feel blessed, reassured—and seen; and that's something everyone needs. The experience of God's presence is bracing and affirming. It lets us know: you matter to . That's why the angels are willing to send sign after sign until we get the message. We are *that* important to God.

Our presence to ourselves can be just as powerful.

Though in the past, we've made promises to ourselves—to make healthier choices for our body; to show up at work on time; to always keep our word—and though we may have broken those promises, we can begin freshly, today, to show up for ourselves.

We can commit to support the choices we make toward better habits, better health, better relationships through our actions—and through conscious daily practice.

I am here: we tell ourselves. When we bring this presence to our relationship with God and the angels, we are saying: *I am here.*

This is a sacred practice—it's showing up with intention to connect, with the expectation of miracles. That, in a nutshell, is faith.

The angels showed me:
When you reach out to us,
we always reach back.

TWO:

The Mystery

A woman walks along a winter beach, eyes downcast, shoulders slumped. More depressed than she's ever been, she thinks of her family, her home, her work. She'd always believed these things would bring her joy—and she's doing her best, sacrificing and working hard to make a go of it. But no matter how she's tried, things haven't worked out that way.

Lost and lonely, she stands at the water's edge, thinking: *Maybe I should just swim out to sea? When everything feels so empty, so meaningless, why go on?*

Suddenly, a man approaches. Where'd he come from? she wonders. The long stretch of beach was deserted a moment ago. She's startled at first, wary. But as the man draws near, she feels the strangest … recognition.

He walks directly to her and invites her to sit on the sand. He's engaging and interesting and somehow, she feels completely at ease in his presence.

Somehow, he senses what she's thinking. She's never shared her feelings and concerns so easily before. It's as if he knows her better than anyone she's ever met, better than she knows herself.

13

Her heart lightens, long forgotten dreams flash into her mind—things that she once thought she'd do and see, pieces of a self she left behind years ago. Though she feels shy about sharing these ideas, he seems fascinated, which encourages her to continue.

After a long, full conversation, they part and she hugs him—*she* who usually holds back, who feels uncomfortable with such intimate exchanges—hugs him!

"Thank you," she whispers.

As he walks away, she turns to face the ocean. She feels better than she's felt since... well, she can't remember when. She breathes in the fresh salt air and her body feels alive, her heart floods with relief and then, she feels it—the thing she thought she'd never feel again—the effervescent sparkle of *joy*. Tears streaming, overwhelmed with gratitude, she turns to thank the mysterious stranger one more time... but where is he?

It's only been a moment. She scans the beach in all directions. Even if he'd run, he couldn't have vanished so quickly. She climbs the dunes, eyes searching acres of sand—and parking lot. But the mysterious stranger is gone.

∞

This story, a composite of many I've read, is happening every day. Maybe it's even happened to you: a stranger appears—on an airplane, beside a hospital bed, in a crowded mall—and offers guidance, a helping hand or a shoulder to cry on. Then, as mysteriously as he or she appeared, the stranger disappears without a trace.

Where did he go? you wonder and, *Who was he?* A rush of heat moves through your body (or a chill runs up the spine) as you realize: My life has been touched by something extraordinary—something I may never fully understand.

14

You see, touch, and feel the presence of the Divine every single day.

Yet if you're like most people, you don't let yourself *believe* it. But *[even though others deny]* every now and then, you have an encounter you can't "reasonably" *[X]* explain, and you wonder: *Could it be?* But you've been trained to doubt your instincts; you edit yourself. "Oh that couldn't have been an angel," you say, echoing the voices of teachers, parents and well-meaning adults who've chorused, "Stop telling stories," "You must have been seeing things," and my personal favorite, "That's just magical thinking." And yet...

You can't let go of your brush with mystery.

You keep coming back to the memory, rolling it over in your mind like sweet candy on the tongue. Enchanted, you keep searching, keep asking and keep noticing. You sense that just under the surface of the "real" world there is a deep flow of mystery.

This curiosity—this *interest* and awareness—is like a glowing chip of moonlight, illuminating the deep caverns of the self where a richer wisdom lives—a wisdom that knows and has always known the truth.

Then, something else happens.

The phone rings and you *know* who's on the line; you think about someone and "coincidentally" bump into them the next day. You make a wish or whisper a prayer and miraculously it's granted. That's all it takes—the moonlit chip in your heart flares with recognition.

This time, or the next, when you can no longer deny that it's real, something inside of you shifts; and this time, when you whisper: *Could it be?* You hear an answer: *Yes...*

Maybe you've already had an experience that deepened your connection to the Divine. Maybe that experience marked the beginning of a journey—through books and classes and conversations with friends, teachers, or members of clergy. Maybe you let others talk you out of it, writing off even your own experience as "just a coincidence."

"Something happened to me... many years ago," the woman in the café tells me.

She was just a kid, barely twenty, driving on four bald tires on the highway, no one else on the road. She heard a loud "bang!" and suddenly, her car was sailing, out of control, right off the road, down an embankment, where it smashed, head on, into a tree.

"I really hit my head," she remembers. "I didn't realize quite how hard at the time. I was dizzy and nauseated... I had to get out. But when I stood up beside my car, I began to swoon. Suddenly this man was there... A tall black man. He was driving a truck, a huge 18-wheeler. It was right there, beside the road. I kept telling him, 'I don't know what happened...' over and over. 'Your tire blew out,' he explained. 'See?' He showed me the tire fragments on the blacktop beside my car. And I understood then."

That's when she passed out cold. Five hours later, she woke up in the hospital.

"Where's the man who brought me in?" she asked doctors, nurses, admitting staff. No one had seen him. There was no record of how she'd arrived.

I tell her this is typical of angelic experience. The angels arrive, lend a hand at an accident scene or hospital bed, then disappear without a trace.

"That doesn't make sense," she says. "It's too...."

"Bizarre, incredible. I know," I say.

"It's just that ... I've always wondered who he was." She pauses. "I've wondered about all of it. I mean, how did I see the shreds of

16

tire on the road at all. When he came, I was standing beside my car, down at the bottom of the embankment? How did I even see his truck?"

"The angels can transcend space and time," I say. "Every day I read a story like yours—if they need a truck, they can make one. They could probably move *us* through space and time if they had to."

"If I believe this," she says, "it becomes a life changing event."

"Don't believe it," I urge. "Test it. Ask for proof."

She laughs. "How could I possibly prove any of this?"

"Ask for a sign—say, 'If this really was an angel, send me a sign'

"I'm afraid to," she shudders. "It's too huge. Too big. If I believe this, it changes everything."

We're like castaways.

This woman has wondered about that event all of her life—for years that chip of moonlight in her heart has been glowing, pulsing her question into the universe: *Could it be?*

I am absolutely certain that God has been answering—pulsing back response after response. But her doubt and fear made it impossible for her to receive any of it.

That's why, this time, the angels sent me.

I hope that doesn't sound arrogant. It's just that after all that I've witnessed, I can no longer pretend this kind of meeting is coincidental. For me, that kind of denial would be a far greater arrogance.

My meeting with this woman was guided—and, as always happens in angel-guided encounters, our meeting rewarded both of us. She received a new kind of answer—a direct, clear explanation delivered by a human being. I received the gift of this story to share with you.

17

As the angels have shown me, they are constantly guiding us, gently and with great love, back to the parallel path. As the woman in the café observed, *that changes everything.*

The angels showed me:
Your longing, your soul questions call
us closer. We are always listening,
always ready to answer.

THREE

My Early Encounters with Angels

I was 26 when I met Joanne. With her flaming red hair and bright blue eyes set in a freckle-splattered face, Joanne was striking and outgoing. On a bright sunny morning, on the sidewalk in front of my apartment building, she walked right up and introduced herself.

We shared many interests: spirituality, stories, science, and film; and we instantly struck up a friendship. But Joanne and I never did 'friend' things: there were no lunches, no shopping and no double dates. All we did was walk around our Forest Hills neighborhood talking about God.

This was new to me. Growing up, I'd had no formal religious training. Though my mother was raised as a Christian, my father an Orthodox Jew, they had stopped practicing their religious traditions by the time they met.

On my family's rare visits to church or synagogue for a wedding, a bar mitzvah or funeral, I didn't understand the meaning behind the rituals. But I savored the quiet mood and the seriousness with which everyone seemed to take the simplest activities—opening a book, singing a prayer, striking a match to light a candle.

I grew up a natural mystic, embedded in the world of nature, deeply attuned to the forest creatures, the wind, the trees.

I was driven by a quest for connection and meaning, with a built-in propensity for science. I asked constantly, "What's this? How does it work?" Often, I received the answers through vivid dreams. Every now and then I'd touch the hem of something that felt meaningful in a different way—a flash of intuition, a feeling of being guided toward something; and a buzz of recognition would sing through me. But without the scaffolding of beliefs and practices that organized religion brings, I was left to meet the world in my own way.

This turned out to be a good thing. It trained me to find meaning from what came to me: the poems and stories my mother read aloud each night, the paintings she took my sisters and me to see in the museums of New York City, the ancient stories my father's family shared at Passover and the High Holy Days.

Though I was bored in school, I loved learning and what I could not find in the classroom, I discovered in <u>books</u>—the beginning of <u>a lifelong pursuit of self-education</u>. I was always reading—up in my room, in the branches of a tree or sitting on the huge boulder at the edge of Lake Tiorati where my family spent several shimmering summers (my father was the camp's director) when I was a girl.

I was desperate to understand, to know, to experience. But my shyness and my youth made me skittish about anything I considered strange—especially anything that might make me appear "weird." I felt different enough already.

So I was skeptical that bright spring morning when Joanne reached up, plucked a fluffy white feather from my hair, and said, "You always have angels around you."

I thought she was nuts. "Or holes in my pillows!" I said.

"No," she said, looking me right in the eye. "It's angels."

She really is strange, I thought. She dresses oddly, lives alone. She doesn't seem to have a job or any other friends. I began to avoid her calls. We drifted apart. She moved away.

I felt guilty then—and I hoped I hadn't hurt her. But I see it differently now. I don't think Joanne was an actual angel (though, who knows?) but I'm certain she was sent to plant a seed, an idea that I'd never considered: *Angels move among us.*

It was around that time when I received my first sign: A single playing card blown across my path on a hot gust of New York City air.

I'd just left my job as a systems analyst to work in the New York office of The Institute for Human Evolution. In the five-week course we offered—DMA: Technologies for Creating—I'd learned to 'tune in' to a person I'd never met and somehow receive useful and meaningful information about his or her life. I was amazed that I could do this, and equally amazed that a stranger could tune into me.

At DMA, I'd learned to ask questions of "The Universe," a vaguely vast *everything* that, I was assured by my teachers, would respond. With my eyes and ears open for that response—which might come from anywhere—I asked my questions. There were so many things I wanted to know but, looking back, I see that the essence of each thing I asked was the same: *God, are you there?*

One day, as I was climbing the stairs of the subway station at 14th Street and Broadway, I received an answer.

Even now, 30 years later, that memory has a special feel to it: the way the card spun in the air, catching my eye before it landed, directly in my path; the way the energy felt—different, electric, charged—setting my senses on high alert.

I picked up the card—*a Two of Hearts*—and turned it over. If this was a message I had no idea what to make of it. I carried the card up to the office where everyone took a turn at guessing its meaning.

For the next few weeks, I kept the card in my pocket, a talisman, a charm that I'd reach for, rubbing the smooth surface between my fingers. Each time I did, the same curious electricity would charge up my spine. This fascinated and frustrated me.

Then, I found another card.

This time, I was *on* the subway, strap-hanging on a crowded rush hour train when I glanced down and saw it lying there, on the black and white tile beside my foot: *the Two of Hearts.*

I picked it up, all of my senses on high alert. It was clear that something was happening—something important. But what it was, I couldn't say. That night, I placed both cards in the top drawer of my dresser. They'd become too precious to carry around.

And then, a few weeks later, on a breezy spring day, as I was sitting on the bed sorting socks, a playing card came soaring in through the open window of our *third floor* apartment and landed on the duvet cover right in front of me.

Yes, *really.*

I picked up my third card, my whole body prickling with excitement and all at once, the enormous, infinite Universe cracked open before me and grinned.

That's how just like that I was pulled across the invisible line between reason and faith; between *talking about* the Divine and having it fly through the window. So began my playful, personal relationship with God—and the angels. 3 cards

The angels showed me:
You live in a call and response universe. When you
call to us, we respond with guidance; our guidance
increases your interest and out of that interest,
you attune more and more, to peace and joy. Your
attunement and interest draws you closer to us.
So it goes in an eternal and infinite circle
of light, love and life.

FOUR:

You Live in a 'Call and Response' Universe

I've heard it said that the angels, looking down upon us from their Heavenly realm, see us — not as physical bodies, but as points of light. It's said that when we are spiritually resonant — engaged and interested, whether we are deep in prayer or on fire with curiosity, creativity or wonder — we light up. The more our interest expands, the "brighter" we appear. They are attracted to that brightness — as we, seeing a single star on a dark night, cannot miss it.

What I must have looked like to the angels then, curiosity pulsing from me like a beacon: *Show me, show me, show me.* It was the simplest of prayers — heartfelt, directed outward. Yet, like many people, I had no clear sense to whom I called.

"To the whole world!" I might have said if asked. It hardly mattered. For each time I called, I was answered in some way, small or stupendous — and each time that happened, my soul responded with a joyful: *Thank you, thank you, thank you!*

In the years that followed, as I raised my children from diapers to grade school, I developed a playful, easy friendship with the eager presence that seemed always just over my shoulder and ready to help with the smallest things.

"Where are my keys?" I'd ask aloud, after searching pocket, purse and countertop. I'd feel a gentle *push,* as if an invisible hand was coaxing, *Turn around* and there were the keys, sparkling on the ground behind my heel.

I'd be driving a familiar route when I'd sense, *Time to change course.* Moments later, as I was breezing along the new route I'd taken, a radio announcer would confirm the traffic snarl I'd avoided. When I lost touch with this presence—as I often did—I felt adrift, like a child lost in the woods—or the department store—without its mother. Gently, I'd feel a tug at the sleeve of awareness, *Don't lose hope, here I am,* and the relief was like coming home.

I referred to this presence by many names: It was *Fairies* who stole and returned my keys; *Traffic Guides* helped me in the car; and the *Universe* had somehow coordinated my experience on the bridge that Thanksgiving. I felt this presence in every part of my life. I knew without a doubt that it was real and I was grateful for its constant support.

But a funny thing happens with miracles: We get used to them.

One day, we're struck through with awe; the next day, we have to get up and go to work. Of course, *this* is the real magic—and invitation of miracles. For as we integrate these marvelous moments into our lives, we come to expect them.

The more you experience the touch of the Divine in your life, the less easily you will slip back into the sleep of unconscious living. It may feel as if you're rediscovering the whole world. You are. You are crossing the bridge from *idea* to direct *experience.* It is then that you will begin to experience, as the Sufi poet Rumi wrote, that *what you seek, is seeking you.*

Deepening

To deepen your connection to the ideas in the previous section:

Speak, write or think this affirmation:
"I live in a call and response universe. When I ask a question, I know that I will receive a response."

Speak, write or think this invocation:
"Please walk beside me. Guide me to the people and practices that will capture my interest and continue to support my unfolding into light."

Contemplate:
The angels showed me: *We want to engage in conscious, active relationship with you. Ask for confirmation of our presence.*

Journal:
What if it were true that I can receive guidance? How might my feelings about 'how it is' change? How might it change me, knowing that I am guided *as truth* (as opposed to a vague possibility)? How might it change the way that I live my life?

Try this:
Writing a conversation with the Divine

Tools: your journal and several different color pens

Imagine that you are having a written conversation with a very talkative angel. If you like, you can close your eyes and imagine yourself inviting this angel to chat with you. The angel agrees and comes close enough to read what you are writing in your journal.

Now, think of a question you'd like to ask. Something you'd like to receive guidance about. (For this first practice, consider not asking about the ONE BIG WORRY that's been driving you crazy for years. Choose something less loaded. You can ask your big question later. This is just a practice session to open the communication channel.)

Now, choose one of the colored pens and write down your question. As you write, imagine your angel moving in to read along.

Switch to a second pen of a different color.

Close your eyes. Take a deep breath and listen. Imagine your angel bending over and dictating the answer. Open to whatever comes—whether it's a flash of imagery, a song, a bunch of nonsense words. Whatever comes, simply record it. Write down whatever comes to mind. Allow the angel to guide your hand as you write. You will know when the answer is complete.

If nothing comes, check in: Are you censoring anything? Perhaps waiting for the 'right answer'? Are you waiting for something that makes sense—or pushing away something you don't want to hear? For example, sometimes this exercise brings guidance that makes people think: That's what I always get! I want something else, something from the angels. What they don't realize is that this repeated phrase or bit of information IS guidance — it has been all along! If you still get no response, set down your pen, close your eyes, and ask: "I am open to receiving guidance in whatever form it comes. Then, walk away. Allow guidance to drift to you in other ways. It may come from a song, an inner feeling, another person. When guidance comes, let yourself hear and receive it.

When you feel the message is complete, thank your angel and put down your pen.

You can play with this exercise further by writing your question with your right hand, which is ruled by the concrete left brain and writing your angels' answer with your left hand, guided by the intuitive right brain.

Grace Note:

In any discussion of the Divine and states of consciousness, a murkiness can develop—it is virtually impossible to talk about matters of the soul with clarity, for it is all impression, feeling, imagery, and subject to the filter of the author's experience.

That said, you will notice that throughout this book, I use the phrases *The Universe* and *The Sea of Miracles* interchangeably. For me, these two labels represent the same thing: a living and responsive wholeness that encompasses all things.

To me, the angels are emissaries sent forth from the Sea of Miracles to keep the world in balance.

To me, each of these is another name for the same thing: The responsive loving universe, created by God.

This concept is a problem for some people, and a few have taken the time to send emails or letters containing quotes from scripture, even photocopied pages of the Bible to set me straight. For those people, let me clarify: I *know* that grace comes from God. In all things, in all ways I give God all the credit for every miracle I experience or witness. I credit God for the sunlight, the water, the food that I eat and the air that I breathe. I also credit God for every interaction with the angels.

The angels are *messengers* of God; but they are not God. I understand, and clearly teach, that the angels are a bridge to that which is too vast for us to meet in its fullness.However, I do not differentiate between God and the angels in my prayers — I just pray. I know that some scriptures have clear guidelines about how to pray and to whom we are supposed to pray.

I encourage you to find your own path to God, to pray in the way that's most comfortable for you. It is your comfort and openness to God's response that is most important — so if following a set of rules brings you to that comfortable openness, by all means follow them.

There are many ways to talk to God and many systems of prayer, meditation and practice. My bottom line: all roads to God are blessed by God; how could they not be when each brings us closer to God?

I do not believe that God minds if I approach the angels with a prayer or a question. God knows my heart – and its intentions. In a universe built of love, designed by love, how could it be otherwise?

II

Attuning to the Angels
–
Intuition
and the
Ways of Reception

Expect Miracles. Expect your every need to be met. Expect the answer to every problem. Expect abundance on every level.

\- Eileen Caddy

The angels showed me:
We want to engage in conscious, active relation-
ship with you and we send signs and guidance
to make contact. You will feel, sense and know us
through your intuition. You will understand our
messages through your imagination.

FIVE

Intuition

It's the middle of the night and a weary college student is driving a dark and lonely highway. His head nods, he yawns. He snaps awake. *I can't keep my eyes open,* he realizes. *I need to sleep.*

Just then, he notices a small, well-lit motel by the side of the road. Longing for a warm bed, a morning shower, he sighs. *I have no money for that.*

Stop anyway, an inner voice urges. Without understanding why, he follows the suggestion. He pulls to the entrance, parks, and steps inside.

The desk clerk looks up. He's an older man and looks oddly familiar. *Tell him,* the inner voice returns. And even though the young man would normally be too shy to ask, he confides his plight.

The kind man pushes a room key across the counter. "Go get some sleep," he says. "You can pay me on the way back."

Grateful, the young man falls into bed. The next morning, on the way out, he grabs the motel's business card, so he can repay the old man's kindness.

A month later, on his next college break, the young man returns to the same town, and, following the address on the business card he's kept in the glove compartment of his car, he pulls into the parking lot. But, to his surprise, the motel is abandoned—boarded up.

Wondering what's happened, he stops in at a convenience store, asking if they know where the owner of the motel might have gone.

"The motel?" the store clerk asks. "That place has been closed for over ten years!"

∞

Nudges, inklings, hunches, gut feelings

Often, the first conscious awareness of guidance comes this way—as an inner nudge, an inkling or gut feeling. An inner pulling urges and you suddenly sense which way to turn, which choice to make. This inner pulling is guidance. It's wisdom. It's part of a conversation—the *response* to a question or prayer. It may come as a flash of inspiration—an idea or mental image accompanied by a rush of feeling, a confident *knowing* that if you follow the guidance, something good will happen.

This feeds your fascination and makes your spiritual experience more charged, more living, more *real*. It changes your perception, making you more open to experimentation. Can I really be talking with angels? you ask. *Yes,* the answer comes: *You can. You are—and so is everyone else.*

Intuition is an inborn sensing, feeling tool that is working all the time to read the energetic quality of people, places and situations. Information is constantly streaming to us through all of our senses —including the intuitive impressions we receive. We receive this information in several ways at once. I call these *The Ways of Reception.*

The angels showed me:

There are many ways to receive guidance.
None is better, 'higher' or more spiritual
than any other. We send you messages in
the way that is easiest for you to receive,
trust and understand.

SIX:

The Ways of Reception
How does guidance come to you?

People who are more visual—artists, for example—will 'see' imagery, receive visions, dreams and signs. Others will receive 'downloads' of sensory information, gut feelings, intuitive flashes, a deep sense of 'knowing.'

Dreamers may receive Technicolor dreams with a full cast of characters and elaborate settings. Scientists may feel guided through an experiment or research project, gathering evidence for what may begin as a hunch or inkling. People who resonate with sound—musicians, orators—may 'hear' guidance, a meaningful song on the radio, a disembodied voice speaking into their ears.

We also receive and read guidance through the body.

Guidance may come through our physical senses—as sight, sound, scent, taste, touch impressions: a tingling at the back of the neck, chills up the spine, the brush of 'something' against the skin. People report the touch of 'unseen hands' that tap them on the shoulder, brush against a face or arm, or even catch them as they fall.

You may experience a sudden rush of sensation, a prickling all over that signals the presence of something or someone nearby. Maybe you've experienced that gut feeling of somehow *just knowing* something, often followed by a flash of imagery or a clear thought.

There are four basic *ways of reception*. None of these ways is better or more advanced than another; none demonstrates a more highly developed connection to the angels. Each is a vital component of your connection to the Divine—and you've been using all of them all of your life.

Seeing/Thinking

Do you 'see' guidance—through vivid dreams, flashes of imagery, or visions? Do you receive downloads of imagery? Do you have the ability to see and read the patterns in stories? Do you have a strong affinity for visual imagery—magazines, paintings, pictures and film? Are you deeply affected by scenes and experiences of natural beauty—sunrises, ocean views, mountain landscapes, the intricate layering of color in a garden or a bird's wings?

Feeling/Sensing

Do you 'feel' guidance—through your emotions or physical senses? Can you sense when someone is lying or uncomfortable? Do you seem to be able to tune into what other people are feeling, and put them at ease? Do you sense the mood of an entire room? Do you make many of your decisions based on gut instincts? Are you especially sensitive to physical stimuli—noise, crowds? Do you talk about reading 'vibes' of people, places or situations? Do you have a strongly developed sense of taste or smell? Are you able to discern the different spices in a sauce or soup?

Hearing

Do you 'hear' guidance—through overheard conversation, songs on the radio, or even the sound of a voice, whispering in your ear? Do you have a strong connection to music, voice, sound? When you walk out of doors, do you always notice the sounds? Can you differentiate bird calls, animal sounds? In orchestral music, do you find yourself able to distinguish the layering of different flows of instrumentation? Do you actually hear voices offering benevolent, loving messages of guidance or encouragement? (It's important to understand that Divine guidance is ALWAYS positive—and would never instruct you to harm yourself or another in any way.)

Knowing

Do you simply 'know' things sometimes, through gut feelings, hunches and other intuitive cues? Do you receive 'downloads' of wisdom or understanding? Do people come to you for guidance, telling you, "I feel seen and understood by you"? Do you have an intuitive sense of how things work—computer systems or complicated machinery, for example? Are you good at putting puzzles together or solving mysteries? Do you tend to see the 'big picture'? Do you inherently understand more than you are being told about politics, family dynamics or systems? Do you see or sense the underlying patterns in things?

Guidance comes from everywhere.

You may receive guidance from TV, radio, songs, cell phones, computers, commercials and email messages. It may come from other people: mysterious strangers, a blurted statement from a friend, an overheard conversation.

Guidance may come from coincidences or events of *synchronicity*—a phone call from the person we were just thinking of, a job offer received at the perfect moment, a romantic encounter that arrives by 'chance' just when we're ready.

Guidance may come from within, as hunches, dreams or imagery. You may receive messages from license plates and street signs.

Messages can come through any portal or person, and you may miss many signs before realizing, "Hey, maybe all of this means something."

Don't worry that you may miss a sign. The angels will keep sending messages until you 'get it'. You can ask for as many signs as you need—and keep asking until you understand and trust the message.

Finally, remember, there's no right way to receive or interpret the guidance you receive; the key is opening to what comes and trusting your instincts as you read the signs.

Grace Note: **Cledons**

About a year before I began working with angel stories, I was sitting in a restaurant, writing in my journal. For weeks, I'd been searching for meaningful work—work where I could apply my way with words in service of helping and uplifting others.

I scribbled down a question: What is my soul's true work? A moment later, all sound fell away and the entire restaurant was silent. I looked up. People were moving around, plates were being delivered and picked up, but for one brief moment, in that strange silence, there was no sound.

I blinked. Across the room, a woman at another table leaned forward and told her friend, "You are an energy healer."

The women were seated all the way across a packed dining room, yet I heard the words as if they'd been spoken directly into my ear. A moment later, the wall of sound returned.

According to author Collette Baron-Reid, the experience I had in the café was a cledon, "a message from Spirit that is innocently and unknowingly delivered to you by someone or something else."

As Baron-Reid explains, "For our ancestors in the Roman Empire, it was common practice to pray to the gods for guidance and then go out into the world to get a message. People expected to get their insight from Apollo through day-to-day interactions; for example, they'd overhear a conversation between strangers at the local market, or a friend would unknowingly deliver a message over dinner."

I've experienced several cledons since that day in the restaurant and each time, I'm struck by the clarity of the sound, the intense certainty that accompanies it. "It's like 'truth amplified,'" Baron-Reid says, "as if Spirit knows exactly what's on your mind and addresses it."

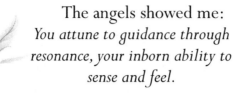

The angels showed me:
*You attune to guidance through
resonance, your inborn ability to
sense and feel.*

SEVEN

Resonance, Energy and Patterns

The word *resonance* means, essentially, 'vibrating with.' It's used to describe the qualities of sound, of musical tones, of voice quality, of electrical or mechanical systems—anything that vibrates.

Resonance is also used to describe the way one thing evokes a response in another. Just as a tuning fork will begin to resonate with another tuning fork, even when they begin at different frequencies, so you will naturally attune to—and vibrate with—the emotional resonance of a touching story on "The Oprah Winfrey Show."

You are already resonating.

Resonance is a built in, automatic sensing skill that you've had (and used) since the day you were born—even before! In fact, the unborn child is already absorbing the rhythmic life of the mother's body—the patterns of heartbeat, respiration and circulation; the patterns of waking and sleeping—using its built-in ability to sense and adjust to resonance.

Once born, you attuned to the resonance and rhythm of family life as your family attuned to your rhythms as well—the sleep-deprived parents of any newborn will attest to that! As you grew, you attuned to the wider rhythms of your community, your friends and extended family. At school you picked up an entirely new set of rhythms, absorbing new codes of conduct, social behavior and dress.

This is 'reading energy" and you've been doing it all of your life!

You did it when you emulated your parents, teachers and the bigger kids on the block. You do it when you pick up the patterns of speech and gesture of sports stars, rock musicians, TV characters and movie icons.

You do it when you adapt to (or react to) the social and political climate at work, at home and in your community. You do it every time you are moved by a guru, religious leader or charismatic politician.

Without really thinking about it, whenever you encounter a new experience or person, you automatically tune into the energy — feeling for rhythm, familiar and compatible (and companionable) energy.

Even our language hints at this when we say, "I get good (or bad) vibes from this," or "We just weren't on the same wavelength." This is energy talk!

Through this same ability to read energy — and to shift into alignment — when we deepen our connection to the angels, to the Divine, the resonance of our entire being — body, mind and spirit — shifts, naturally and easily, to align with the vibration of Divine love and light.

People ask me...
Is this guidance? (How to know)

When I encounter students at the beginning of their spiritual journey, they often ask me: Is this guidance? Is it angels? They describe a sensation in their body, an image they've perceived, a voice they heard as they awoke that morning, a dream they had last week. Always, I turn them back to their own instincts. "What do YOU think it is?" I ask, urging them to tune in to their own blossoming intuition.

I know this is frustrating. They want quick answers; they want to *know* what they're experiencing is real. But I've learned to resist the urge to solve the mystery for them. Leaving questions open helps people turn to their own guidance, and that is the ultimate goal of all spiritual paths.

The early stages of awakening—the brightening of interest and deepening of attunement—are for experimentation, for wiggling our toes in the spiritual sand and feeling the grains against our skin.

This is the perfect time for experimentation with signs. It's a time of asking questions and waiting patiently for the answers to come; of learning to hold our minds and hearts open to receive them in whatever form they come. It's a time of beginning faith, as we test the Universe: Will I receive an answer this time? And this time? And this time?

I encourage my clients to get playful with the angels. "Ask for more signs," I tell them. "Ask for a sign you can't miss." I suggest that they start a guidance journal and record the signs and synchronicities that come. Playing with your angels can bring a sense of childlike wonder and joy.

It's like a game, in which you ask a question of the universe and watch for signs all day—and signs will come all day long. The angels are as playful as we are. As my radio co-host Janet Paist has observed, "The angels often have similar 'personalities' to our own—delivering guidance in a form and manner that we're comfortable receiving."

Try this:
Sensing Guidance Through Your Body

Which one should I choose?
Use this technique for yes/no questions or any time you need to choose between two things.

1) Think of a choice you have to make. For this practice exercise, choose something simple. Use a situation or decision where you have only two options: Yes or No; This or That.

2) Hold both hands out before you, palms facing up.

3) Close your eyes.

4) Imagine the first option sitting on the palm of your right hand. (Don't worry about *how* to visualize it, just imagine a word or image that represents that option simply forming in your mind's eye and floating down into the palm of your right hand.)

5) Now imagine the second option forming on the palm of your left hand.

6) Sit quietly, letting yourself feel the weight of each choice. Let yourself feel any body sensations that come up. Does one hand feel heavier than the other? Does one hand feel warmer, cooler, more 'bright?' (There's no right or wrong way to feel this. Each of us has our own set of body sensations that we use every day to feel our way into experience. Just feel what *you* feel.)

7) When you have a clear sense of what each option feels like, ask yourself: which choice feels *better?* Which choice feels more resonant with who I am? (You may experience this as one choice feeling heavier, more like a burden while the other feels less weighty. You may experience it in a different part of your body—the belly, the gut, the chest. Only you will know. Let yourself know. Which choice feels better?)

8) Make a note of the response. *This is guidance.*

9) Notice what happens when you follow the guidance you receive; notice what happens when you don't.

The angels showed me:
*You live in a dynamic, living
Sea of Miracles — an interconnected
universe composed of love and light.*

EIGHT

Light, Love, Life Energy

We are just beginning to understand how the world is made. Breakthroughs in science have demonstrated that at the atomic level, the same energy that flows through the cells and tissues of your body also flows through the world around you.

We now also know that the same essential energy that burns in the sun also pulses the tiny heart of a bird; the same energy that lives in a daffodil bulb sleeping under the snow is also in me — and in you!

What is even more amazing, we are beginning to discover that this same energy also comprises your consciousness and even, perhaps, the living, flowing world of the Divine.

As Mystics learn to explain their perceptions in more scientific terms and scientists learn to measure energetic phenomena ever more acutely, the evidence is building for what our faith traditions have been teaching all along: *Consciousness moves through and across matter.*

In other words: thoughts create effects in the physical world and, by inference, so may divine guidance, intuition and prayer!

One thing is certain, we live in an interconnected universe.

One universe, made of one oceanic sea of energy. Traditional Chinese Medicine has been working with this universal animating energy for thousands of years (they call it *Qi or Chi*) to balance, strengthen and heal the body.

Ayurvedic Medicine and Hindu tradition are aware of and work with this energy, too. They call it *Prana,* the life sustaining force that pervades all living organisms and the universe. But the concept of animating energy is not exclusive to Eastern tradition. It is *Christ Consciousness,* Light and *Holy Spirit.* We find it in Jewish mystical texts as *Shekinah,* divine Spirit manifesting as a guiding presence.

In all mystical traditions, this universal animating energy is referred to as *light,* as *love,* as the animating energy of *life* itself.

This energy is:

- **Pure, whole and essential.** It is love at its fullest, inspiration at its clearest, life force, bursting toward expression. As the angels showed me: *The animating force of all things is love—and one day, your scientists will prove this. This energy is the white light of All That Is/God; it is the most powerful force in the Universe and it is, at the same time, the most gentle and loving.*

- **Intelligent.** This *intelligence* animates our bodies, holds our furniture together, germinates the plants in our gardens—even the air, which seems empty, is a sea of intelligent, interactive, living energy. Buddhists and yoga teachers refer to this energy as *awareness.*

- **Running through the body** along a series of channels known as *meridians* in Chinese Medicine and as *nadis* in Ayurveda—

ebbing and flowing with the general health of the body.

- **Running through the earth** along powerful streams of energy called *ley lines*. Sensing this, our ancestors built some of the world's most revered and beautiful cathedrals at points where the energy could be felt in a particularly powerful way. (You can learn more about this by searching the word "Ouivre" and/or the words "ley lines" on the Internet.)

This light, love, life energy is in all things and can take any form.

As Albert Einstein himself explained, "All matter is energy," and in our material world the objects that we see and touch, as well as the earth beneath our feet, the buildings we inhabit and all of the plants and animals are composed, at the essential level, of this energy.

This light, love, life energy organizes itself into form by flowing into patterns.

These patterns, or *fields,* weave together to form every object in our physical world. In fact, according to the angels, the very ground on which you walk is made of love!

These fields are like blueprints, a kind of energetic DNA. So the pattern (or field) of a rose tells the love, light, life energy to flow into the form that we recognize as 'rose.' Just as the pattern called 'star' directs the flow of light, love, life energy into that form. These patterns have consciousness and intelligence.

Some of these fields form your body, some form the plants in your garden and some of these fields form the angels. Taken together, all of these fields, all of this flowing energy, forms a vast web of interconnectivity, an enormous *everything* that includes every object, liquid, gas, idea, dream—even our thoughts—everything that has ever existed.

Buddhists call this interconnected universe Indra's Net.

They imagine it studded with glittering jewels or pearls—with each gem tied to every other; and every jewel is a holographic reflection of every other jewel so that everything that exists reflects and includes every other thing that exists. For all is one.

Now imagine this: Through every strand and jewel of our interconnected universe, the light, love, life energy is flowing. Like the invisible energy that we tap into with our cell phones—or like "The Force" in Star Wars films—this energy is an enormous everywhere field accessible to anyone who has the tools to use it.

Yes, yes—this is all very interesting but what does it have to do with angels?

Everything. Angels are energetic beings, literally composed of Divine light. This light is the same energy that animates the body, the same love that fills the heart, the same energy that inspires the mind. Like everything else in the universe, the angels are *made of* light, love, life energy.

Grace Note:
A Way Of Thinking About Resonance

Just before coming to work at the DMA office, I worked as a Telecommunications Specialist/Systems Support Analyst for Wang Labs, a pioneer in the office automation industry. It was my job to teach my clients—bankers, insurance brokers and lawyers—to use the strange new personal computer systems that were appearing on their desks.

This was back before cell phones, before email, before the Internet. I still remember the awe with which we watched a demonstration of the Qwix—one of the first fax machines. Though today, we easily transmit documents by email, back then the idea felt like magic or something out of Star Trek!

Until then, if we'd wanted to send a document to another office we had to send it by mail or messenger. Now, we were translating the same document into pulses of energy (sound, and later, light) and transmitting it across vast distances in seconds.

During my training, I learned that in all data communication, it was important to establish a 'protocol'—a common frequency and language—before data could be transmitted. There had to be *resonance*.

So we sent out a 'handshake'—a series of beeps and blips that the receiving system could read, interpret and respond to. If you've ever telephoned someone and been greeted by their fax machine and its series of high-pitched beeps and blips, you've witnessed this. Their fax machine is asking for the basic information and needs to establish a connection.

What protocol (language) is the first system speaking? Which protocol (language) does the second system require?

When we open our connection with the angels—and with God, we are doing essentially the same thing: We send out a prayer. it is received and read, and a response is sent back to us in a protocol (language) of signs, symbols, and intuitive blips and bleeps tailored to resonate with our particular system. If we don't receive the response, another is sent—again and again until contact has been made.

The angels showed me:
*You are never disconnected from us. The Sea of
Miracles surrounds, holds and cradles you — it
flows to you and through you. All that you are
and all that you do is an expression of this
flowing sea of light, love, life energy.*

Meditation:
Sea of Miracles

**Go to http://amyoscar.com/sea-of-miracles-meditations/ to watch a
video or listen to the MP4 recording, or read the text below.**

You are living at the center of a responsive, loving universe
of light—a gently moving, undulating, shimmering ocean of
energy, gentler and less perceptible than mist; yet more powerful
than any force on Earth.

This guided meditation is designed to give you a direct experience of your connection with that powerful Sea of Miracles. It
will be most effective if you approach it with an open mind and
let yourself drop into the fullness of the experience.

∞

Find a quiet place where you won't be disturbed for about 10
minutes. Close your eyes.

Take a deep breath.

Imagine that you're floating at the center of a shimmering globe of light. A golden bubble of clear, welcoming white light that completely surrounds and enfolds you. The bubble is safe, structurally sound and secure. You are safe here—completely comfortable and firmly but gently held.

Now, take another deep breath.

Notice that this light is mixed into the air that you breathe. Imagine that you can draw the light in with your breath and feel it filling your lungs and flowing through your body, bathing and brightening every cell with clarity—a gentle rich bath of light.

This light is not just visible light, it is also vital chi, the energy of life itself.

Feel this light move from your chest, down into your belly, your pelvic area and buttocks.

Feel the light circulate up your spine, into your head, flowing down from your forehead across your cheeks, through your neck and into your shoulders, arms and hands. Feel it flow through your limbs—down your legs and into your feet.

Feel the light circulating through you and to you, filling your body with brightness and clarity and peace.

This light is not just visible light- and life-giving chi, it is also, love. Pure unconditional love. Take another deep breath and allow that awareness to fill you.

Now bring your awareness back to the bubble around you. It begins to expand, growing wider around you, you still at the center. See it expand until you can no longer see its edges, until you are floating at the center of a living universe of light, of life, of love.

You are made of the same substance, shimmering living light. Your body is made of this light. Your thoughts and emotions are all expressions of this light.

Breathe.

Imagine that a presence begins to emerge from this sea — a being composed of light itself; emerging the way that a bit of cloud might push up and out of a larger cloud. Notice that this presence is both a part of the sea of light and yet, also differentiating itself from the sea, so that you can observe and interact with it.

As it emerges, a wave of gentle peace pours through you. Know with every fiber of your being that you are safe, you are loved.

Watch as the light begins to form into a ball of white light that dances playfully around the room. Watch it change form, stretching into the familiar shape of a person — a person entirely made of light.

Look into its eyes and experience the flood of the most pure, unconditional acceptance you have ever experienced.

You are standing in the presence of an angel.

This angel has been called to you, by you, right now. It has come because you called it forth with your curiosity, your simple wish to know — and to experience — *more*.

You've called this angel into form with your interest. That was enough.

Ask your angel if it has anything to tell you. Allow yourself to receive whatever message your angel has to share. The message may come as words, as feelings, as thoughts, as physical sensations. Allow it to come in whatever way that it comes.

Know that you can receive the message—and allow it to come. Know that you will continue to receive this message and others, in the future. There is no urgency. Relax and allow whatever comes to come.

When you've received the message, thank your angel in whatever way you like. Know that your angel is with you always. You can call on your angel at any time—for any reason. Even if all you want or need is a sign of its presence.

In the coming days, allow yourself to see and experience signs of your angel's constant presence.

Now, watch your angel recede—fading like cloud into cloud, white light diffusing and spreading into a brilliant brightness that fills every corner of the room.

As the light fades, bring your attention back to the sea, the living sea of light, life and love pulsing around you.

Out of this sea, all of life, all that is, is formed. Everything is part of the living sea of miracles, made of the same essential stuff as the angels. So are you – and so is everyone else.

Take one last deep cleansing breath, bringing your awareness back to your body.

Wiggle your fingers and toes. Open your eyes.

Deepening

To deepen your experience of the ideas in this section:

Affirmation (speak, write or think):
"I am becoming more and more able to feel, sense and know the resonance of energy in all things."

Invocation (speak, write or think):
Please open my heart to attune to resonance with light, love, and life energy. Help me to experience your presence in my life.

Consider:
What the angels showed me: *You receive guidance through all of your senses. Watch for signs of our presence in your thoughts, feelings, bodily sensations; watch for visual signs, auditory signs, smells, tastes, gentle brushes or sensations of soft pressure against your skin.*

Journal:
Think back to times when you may have experienced guidance already. How did it come to you? How did it feel? What did you make of it? Did you tell anyone? What did they say?

III

Reading the Divine

–

Interpreting Guidance
with Symbolic Sight

"When the soul wants to experience something she throws out an image in front of her and steps into it."

–Meister Eckhart

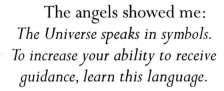

The angels showed me:
The Universe speaks in symbols.
To increase your ability to receive
guidance, learn this language.

Reading the Divine

The Divine is a poet with a wild broad brush—and, as you will see, the angels often use the same symbolic language poets use to deliver its messages.

We are programmed to understand and receive messages this way. Artists are particularly attuned to symbolic language and philosophers, poets, and painters have embedded them into works of literature and visual art for centuries. But even the least "artistic" person can learn to recognize and interpret symbols. When you learn to interpret the symbolic messages the angels send, the whole world becomes your mirror. The angels will paint messages on the sky, in the forests and streams and whisper messages in the wind. Your ancestors, the native peoples of all lands, understood and used this ability to receive information about their health, relationships and communities.

So can you. In fact, you already are using it any time you ask, "What does this mean?" This section is designed to help you learn to work more deliberately with your inborn ability to read the signs the angels send.

NINE:

Interpreting guidance with Symbolic Sight

When my children were in middle school, I began to feel unsettled. Caught between work and family, between wanting to please everyone and needing, desperately, to express myself, I felt trapped. In our small, crowded house, there was one available space—the kitchen table—and every time I found the time to sit down to write (or just to think) someone would walk through, needing my attention.

Somehow, or so it seemed to me, I'd created a home—and a lifestyle—that supported everyone in the family in their creative work except me. *Is there no room for me in my life?* I wondered.

My marriage felt strained as my husband and I, both artists, wrestled for the freedom to pursue our creative interests, each blaming the other for lack of support.

Frustrated, we scheduled a couples' counseling session with a therapist to help us sort out our feelings. But on our way there, we began to argue so bitterly that I asked—well, honestly, I demanded—that he pull the car over so I could walk the rest of the way to her office.

Emotions swirling, head down, I walked slowly, hoping to calm down before arriving. I'd traveled about a quarter mile when, *What's that?* I wondered. With so much on my mind, I don't know what made this particular piece of roadside debris, buried in snow and mud, catch my attention.

I bent to retrieve it. It was a small refrigerator magnet —the image, a pink and white ballerina. One of its feet had broken off and it was scuffed and scratched—and the moment I saw what it was, I was swept with a deep wave of memory—and grief.

I was ten years old, and I was going to be a ballerina. I loved everything about ballet—my black leotard and powder pink tights, my soft pink leather slippers, the way my body felt as I leapt across the polished wood floor of the studio.

Most of all, I loved my teacher: Misha, a real ballerina, who pronounced the exotic new language of ballet—tour jeté, plié, arabesque—with a clipped Russian accent.

It was the day we'd be graduating to toe shoes and I could barely contain my excitement. For days, I'd been practicing—standing on my toes at home, on the sidewalk all the way to school. But first, there was a test—just a little review of the steps we'd been practicing all year.

I knew it cold. We lined up at the barre—and then, it was my turn. I leapt! I spun—joy bursting from my body like sunlight. Misha smiled. "Excellent!" she said, clapping her hands.

After each girl had taken her turn, Misha examined our feet. One at a time, we sat beside her on a long wooden bench and she took our feet in her hands, turning and bending them. Awaiting my turn, I scanned the stack of pink boxes containing the satin toe shoes. I loved the sound of the chalky thump-thump-thump against the wooden floor as the older girls danced. I couldn't wait to lace the pink satin ribbons up my calves.

But, "Your feet are deformed," Misha said firmly. "You'll never be a ballerina." I felt as if I'd been set on fire. Shattered, I walked back to the barre. There was no arguing. Nothing could be done. The next little girl took my place on the bench.

Even now, remembering this, my throat closes with sorrow as if it were happening today.

I remember my mother coming to pick me up. I remember pushing past her, running to the car, choking back tears all the way home. "What's wrong, sweetheart?" she kept asking. But I couldn't answer her. I sat, silent, frozen solid.

I never wore my ballet clothes again, never returned to class. Though later, I tried other forms of movement — jazz, modern, and later, disco — something inside of me had broken, a body-soul connection I would not reclaim until, forty years later, standing at the side of a busy road with a broken, mud-covered ballerina magnet in my hand, I received a message of healing: *You've left your dreams by the side of the road too long. Let yourself dance.*

I took the magnet and the story it had given me into our counseling session. That was the day that my marriage began to heal — the day I told my husband, "I have to dance," and he said, "Of course you do."

∞

Most people are aware that symbols often show up in dreams. But did you know that symbolic messages cross into our waking lives?

When a client presents me with a story like this, we examine the details of the story as if it were a dream. This helps us bring the symbolic elements into focus.

We take every object in the story and ask, Why is this here? and let it speak. In my story, the elements we'd examine might be the car, the snowy road, the ballerina magnet that triggered a cascade of memory and healing. In a kind of story alchemy, each of the objects we encounter in the physical world can act as prompts for spiritual unfolding that is asking to emerge.

Reading the world in this way opens a new 'eye' that 'sees' with all of your senses. Now, the rush of wind through the trees reminds you of the need to refresh a relationship; the falling autumn leaves may symbolize a life cycle or the passage of time, each snowflake that melts against your windshield becomes a symbol of your own precious and unique beauty.

The symbols I see help me put words to the sense impressions I receive — providing imagery that my clients can use to build their own pictures of the situation.

I look out of the window as a woman is telling me about her strict father and feel my attention drawn toward a tree, bending in the wind. "Could you imagine yourself bending away from his anger without breaking?" I suggest, "Would a more pliable, flexible attitude toward your father help him be less rigid with you?"

Once, as a male client was describing a painful and difficult situation at work, I found my attention drawn to the way that the leaves were clogging a curbside drain, causing flooding. When I mentioned the image and remarked that water is a symbol for the emotions, my client began to weep.

He told me how overwhelmed he felt, how his frustration at the work that piled up on his desk each day was 'spilling over' into his relationship with his wife and son.

The pressure was backing up in other areas, too, he told me. It was blocking the flow of his creative energy — just as those leaves gathering in the drain were blocking the flow of the rainwater.

The metaphor of the blocked drain allowed him to acknowledge and quickly release his pent-up emotions. Now, because he had seen and understood his situation, he was able to move toward resolution.

The angels showed me:
We stream guidance to you using energy,
symbols and messages; you have a built-in
ability to receive and interpret this guidance as
impressions, imagery and intuitive knowing.

TEN

The Imaginative 'Organ' of the Psyche

The Divine speaks in symbols, for symbols are the language of the soul. We interpret this language with the imagination.

Because I am able to see, intuitively, the architecture of the psyche, I perceive the imagination as a non-physical 'organ'. This organ exists in a specific space in the psyche and does a particular job — like each of the organs in your body.

We use this organ to create and interpret images, both mental and visual. We use it to recognize faces and to translate black marks on paper into meaningful words.

We also use it to make meaning out of literature, poetry, film and fairy tale; to understand and invent metaphor, and to write and tell stories. We use it every single day, all day, in countless ways.

When a psychotherapist helps you to understand a dream or a minister explains the larger meaning behind the stories in the Bible, when a scientist explains a theory or an astrologer interprets your birth chart, they, too, are using the imagination.

But, before we continue, let's make sure we aren't confusing the inventions of the imagination—fantasy, lies, illusions—with the function of the imagination—interpretation, symbolic sight, creative problem solving.

The signs and messages the angels send are not illusions, not inventions. They are concrete physical and intuitive material that we receive and then interpret using the imaginative gifts of story and symbolic sight. In this way, we make meaning out of the events of our lives.

The crow that healed my depression

After my second child was born, I struggled with post partum depression. One day, a crow with a broken wing landed on my porch. Moved by its plight, I began to feed it. It surprised me that the crow, a wild bird, didn't seem frightened by me. In fact, it moved closer each time I came outside. I never told anyone about my winged visitor and one day, my husband, alarmed to find it on the porch, chased it away with a broom. When I found out, I cried for an hour. But of course, my husband hadn't meant any harm. When I explained that the crow, unable to fly, was my friend, he smiled. "But it *can* fly," he said. When I went outside, I found the crow sitting on a branch about twenty feet from the porch.

It never came back to the porch—and I stopped feeding it. Still, my friend stayed nearby, visiting that branch all spring. When I came outside, it would fly closer. It was only later that I realized that helping the crow to heal had also healed me.

Ever since, crows have been a symbol for me—a totem, representing the generous love with which nature holds us in the embrace of the Divine.

A pool of ancient wisdom

Sometimes, students ask me: What if I receive symbols I don't completely understand? I tell them: Ask for more guidance—and search the Internet for meaning. There is a whole world of meaning at our fingertips. If you encounter a symbol in a dream or waking experience, simply type the words "symbolic meaning of <name the symbol>" into a search engine like Google.com.

The Internet has become a virtual pool of symbolic ancient wisdom—a mirror of the "collective unconscious" identified by Carl Jung, out of which all cultures may have derived their symbols and stories.

You will not receive guidance that frightens you.

For example, the first time I read a letter from a woman who'd awakened from a sound sleep to find an enormous angel beside her bed, I shuddered. Good heavens! I hope that doesn't happen to me! Now I understand that it never will—I don't need that kind of high-drama guidance. The angels have communicated as much, and just as powerfully with me, using a single feather.

What I mean is, each of us has a personal style, an energetic signature—a way of meeting the world. The angels know this and tailor their messages to meet us the most comfortable way they can.

So, if you're a practical joker, don't be surprised if your angels are too!

If you prefer no-nonsense communication, your angels will deliver straightforward and clear messages you can't miss. If you have a strong connection to words and language as I do, the angels will use license plates, overheard conversations, street signs and other 'word" signs. If you watch a lot of TV or love to listen to the radio, rest assured the angels will use broadcast media to get their messages to you.

The angels don't do this to be coy or cute or to trick you. They customize their communication style because they want you to *receive* their messages; and the easiest, most effective way to ensure that you do is to work with the objects, people and experiences that are familiar to you.

Grace Note: **Seeing Light**

Some people receive, as guidance, flashes of color or light—often in the peripheral vision. Some people can see the 'aura' or 'light body,' a measurable energy field that surrounds each of our physical bodies.

[handwritten: Doreen Joey]

When I began working with large groups, in the 1980s, I was leading a section of the DMA Teacher Training where participants were doing a closed-eye meditation. I was sitting on the stage in a captain's chair with an open notebook on my lap, and reading the meditation into a hand-held microphone. The lights were dimmed.

The meditation led participants into a deep state of relaxation and visualization. One afternoon, I glanced up at the group and saw, hovering over their heads, a beautiful white blanket of light. It looked like fog but it was glowing and it moved, undulating as if breathing, as if pulsing…a blanket of white light.

I saw that white light blanket several times after that. I look for it whenever I lead a meditation. It's not always there. But when it is, it still stuns me with its beauty—and its *reality.*

Experiences like this showed me to trust my senses. I did not understand it but I saw it. I could not explain it scientifically but I could work with it. Like breathing, which my physical body performed without my conscious intention, attention or effort, my physical senses and my intuition are always working.

The angels showed me:
Guidance is always streaming toward you;
it's up to you to open to receive it and to
learn to interpret what comes.

ELEVEN

A Personal Language of Symbols and Signs

As signs and symbols flowed into my life and my dreams, there were many books and websites to help me untangle and interpret their meaning. Through research, I learned that some of the symbols I was seeing bore archetypal meanings—broad, universal themes that could be applied for everyone.

Once I'd read descriptions of the general meaning of a symbol, I discovered that most of them bore personal meaning, as well.

Water, a classic dream symbol of the unconscious and also, the emotions, was also, for me, a symbol of the loss that I felt over the passage of time.

How does one figure this out?

Deer, which often symbolize gentleness, were, for me, an invitation to the parallel path that increasingly beckoned.

And then there were the bees…

When I started working with angel stories, bees started to appear in my dreams. In one dream, I *was* a bee—and I was led, ceremonially, up a spiraling path inside a hive. After a bee dream, I'd wake up inspired, renewed and eager—as if I'd been through a rigorous training program. Through my research, I learned that for the ancient Egyptians, bees were a powerful symbol. To them, bees were alchemists—capable of transforming the sun's golden rays into golden sweetness. In Hinduism, the gods Indra, Krishna and Vishnu are referred to as, "the nectar born." In Christianity, Jesus is referred to as "honey in the rock."

Many cultures across the globe liken the experience of coming into resonance with Divine energy with the buzzing community life of the hive and the rich, sticky sweetness of honey. What intrigued me even more was that some part of me had been aware of this symbolic resonance *before* I'd done the research.

Then, I mentioned my bee dreams to my mother...

"That makes sense," she said. "The bees have been with you since you were a baby." When I said I had no idea what she meant, my mother waved a hand. "Of course you do," she said. Then she reminded me...

"One morning, when you were no more than a year old, I came out of the back door of your grandmother's house and there you were, sitting in the garden with a crown of bees—a buzzing, living wreath of bees—completely surrounding your head. You seemed to be listening to them," she remembered. "Just sitting there peacefully, as they buzzed around your head."

Not one bee had stung me, she recalled. "Not until I came running outside and grabbed you. Then, they stung us both. But I was surprised how few stings you had. One or two... I on the other hand, had plenty!"

That story led me to consider other, equally intriguing bee encounters I'd had at 7, at 12, at 27. But no bee encounter was more striking than this:

I was 35, standing in the kitchen savoring the quiet as both of my children were, for once, asleep at the same time. I was standing at the counter, sipping a glass of water when I heard something buzz up behind me.

I turned. A bee had entered the open back door and it was desperately trying to escape. I watched it dart from kitchen to living room to dining room. Banging itself against the windows, zipping to the ceiling.

I didn't want to get stung. But I did want to help. I could open a window, or trap it gently in a paper cup and carry it outside.

Suddenly, the bee made a, well, a bee line, directly toward my face! I pulled back, wincing. But just before it hit me, it stopped, hanging in mid-air in front of my forehead.

I could feel the bee kind of 'staring' at me.

Gulping, I said, "Hello." I said it out loud — glad no one else was in the kitchen to witness this, the moment when I lost my mind. But I tell you, that bee answered me! In a flash, I received a mental image that I can only describe as a map. It was also a question. Somehow, the bee was 'telling' me: I'm lost. Can you help me get out of here?

In the slowed-down time (a kind of suspended animation) in which these experiences often occur I 'answered,' forming a mental image of the route the bee would need to follow to find the door and then, 'transmitting' it, through the center of my forehead back to the bee.

The bee hung a moment longer; then it flew off, following the exact pattern I'd 'sent' it and sailed through the door.

It was at that moment that I realized: *That bee just taught me how to send messages with my mind!*

∞

[handwritten note: do only clv. see the aura?]

Rudolf Steiner wrote that bees are attuned to high frequency energy and might be able to 'see' it—perhaps the way clairvoyants see auras of light around our bodies. When we raise the frequency of our own vibration through meditation, spiritual practice or prayer, bees may see or sense this 'sweetening' in us and be attracted to investigate.

In my studies, I learned that bees, animals and other insects can and do pick up on the energetic vibrations that we humans send out—and that these vibrations are sent through our sixth chakra, located in the center of the forehead.

This helped me to speculate about my childhood crown of bees. Perhaps it was a conversation—an exchange of 'sweetness' between a child, whose thoughts—like the thoughts of all children—were naturally pure and 'sweet.' I sensed also that, somehow, my early encounter was an invitation into relationship.

From my dreams into my waking life

Now they had my attention, the bee signs increased. I received bee greeting cards and found bee-decorated objects on my desk at work. I switched on the car radio just as a discussion of honeybees was beginning, a friend, completely unaware of my bee connection, sent me a copy of a book connecting bees with Divine guidance.

One day, I mentioned all of this to my friend at work and she laughed. "You're a bee priestess!" she proclaimed, suggesting that *Bee* might be a *totem*—a representative from the natural world working with the angels to deliver guidance.

I was pondering that idea an hour later as I pulled onto the Palisades Parkway headed for home. Suddenly, a car cut in front of me. Stunned, I read its license plate: *Chakra 7*.

I knew that the seventh chakra, the energy center located at the crown of the head, is our bio-energetic connection to Divine energy. Laughing, I realized I'd just received another message, one that con-firmed my energetic connection with the bees—and with guidance itself!

how?

what was the message?

Spirit is in constant conversation with us

You can find your symbolic language by recording your dreams, by reviewing memories from childhood through the present. Look for repeating themes and patterns and for symbolic *totem animals* like my crows, deer and bees.

You, too, have your own symbolic dream language. Becoming aware of the symbols that resonate with you—and the kind of listening you are most attuned to—your *way of reception*—will help you more clearly receive and interpret guidance.

How?

IV

Patterns of Guidance
–

Animals, Birds and Butterflies
Signs from Beyond
Angel Taxis
Protection
Voices
Mysterious Strangers

Patterns of Guidance

Ask the angels,
*Please send me clear signs that illuminate
my personal symbols. Help me to see and to
understand them.*

There is great potential in the signs the angels send. But only if we are open to receive them: We can receive signs with a detached, "well, isn't that something?" or we can allow them to penetrate us, to spark us, to make us think, and to open our hearts.

Signs can remind us that we're part of something bigger than ourselves—something that is calling us back to our *own* true nature as spiritual and physical beings, divinely woven into the web of creation. Even now, as I write these words, a bird swoops, back and forth, outside my window, confirming—again—my connection to all that is.

This section will help you to recognize the many kinds of signs the angels send and to trust the signs you receive.

The angels showed me:
We often send messages through the animals,
birds and insects of your world. Any creature
can be a Divine messenger.

TWELVE:

Animal Guidance

Animals are included as symbolic messengers in the sacred texts (and daily lives) of many ancient cultures including the Celts, Native Americans, Middle Eastern and Asian people. Lions, lambs, eagles, doves (and other animals) are referenced repeatedly in the Old Testament, New Testament, the Koran—even the Chinese Horoscope.

When animals appear in a dream or waking experience, draw upon the cumulative wisdom of these traditions to interpret its meaning. Here are some examples:

- **The animal's name:** We might simply look at the *name* of the animal. For example, a deer may represent a "dear one." A bee could be a message to "Just Be."

- **The animal's qualities:** We may look to an animal sign for its *qualities,* in which case the appearance of a dream deer might represent shyness, gentleness or trust. A snake might be a symbol of transformation. A wolf might represent an invitation to explore our wildness.

- **The animal's symbolic meaning:** We may tap into the collective pool of imagery with a quick search of the Internet. There, we'll find references to deer in myth, fairy tale and film. As we read through the references that come up, we feel for resonance, for meaningful connections.

- **The animal's role is a meaningful story:** When I had several dreams of deer and hearts, I learned, from the Internet, that deer were often referred to as 'harts' and that in the mythology of many cultures the deer is considered a messenger or representative of the Divine. Of course, dreaming of deer and hearts could also bear the simpler message: "Dear hearts."

- **The animal's personal association to you:** A deer may indicate a "dear" one. A butterfly may be a sign indicating heightened intuition, a visitation from a lost loved one or a message telling you: Focus, right now!

- **Your intuitive knowing:** If you receive a sign from the animal kingdom, trust your intuition. What thoughts flashed through your mind when the sign arrived? These flashes of insight are guidance.

Animal guidance isn't just symbolic; it can be practical — even life saving!

Some animals truly are angels on Earth. I've read countless stories of people being led to safety or to the aid of another person by animal guides. A dog may lead us back onto a forest trail; a cat may scratch at the door, warning of smoke.

Any animal can help us — and I've heard stories about rabbits, deer, egrets, foxes, wolves, even bears, serving, in one way or another, as spiritual guides for people.

Winged Messengers

As my sensitivity to guidance increased, I experienced many encounters with winged messengers: The hummingbird that hung in front of my face in the garden one morning, staring into the center of my forehead in front of my astonished husband; the birds that swooped in front of the car as a warning to slow down.

There were also the feathers...

Ever since I was a young girl, my mother had collected feathers —bluebird feathers in the back yard, stiff speckled feathers on the beach. So many that she'd started working them into the collages and paintings she made.

When I started to work with the angels, I found feathers in the most remarkable places—in public bathrooms, on the floors of the cafés where I write, inexplicably clinging to my clothing, on the passenger seat of my car.

One day, I went to the kitchen to make a cup of tea and returned to find a large, stiff white feather on my keyboard. If my husband or one of the children had been home, I could have shrugged it off as a sweet gesture from them. But I was alone in the house, working on an angel story.

The people I work with find feathers, too. "Watch for your feather!" I warn them when we begin a project together—for a feather always comes. When I told a new editor this, she fell silent for a moment. "Amy," she said, "It happened already. Today, when my son stepped off the kindergarten bus, he handed me a feather. 'I got this for you, Mommy,' he said."

Feathers are a kind of shorthand that the angels often use to quickly communicate, "Good job!" or "We are with you," or to affirm a choice we feel uncertain of, with a resounding, feathered, "Yes!"

If you visited my home, you'd find feathers sticking out of the edges of mirrors and photo frames. There are so many—found in the most unusual places—that I started piling them in bowls at the entrance of our home.

These feathers are a symbol of the many stories I've read. Like the stories, each feather is uniquely beautiful, each a reminder of the way the angels cross between the physical and non-physical world.

The angels showed me:
You receive much information
through dreams. In sleep, you are less
defended, more open.

THIRTEEN:

Angel Dreams

Angel dreams feel different from regular dreams—more 'real', more loaded with meaning. Angel dreams may arrive with Technicolor imagery and full story lines. You may hear your name or a meaningful phrase whispered as you open your eyes. You may wake up remembering one powerful image or idea that changes everything.

The white owl

When our dear family friend, Edith, passed away, my mother felt guilty that she'd neglected to keep up the friendship in the past few years. One evening, she called to tell me, "When I went to sleep last night, I felt agitated and sad. I was crying a little, thinking about Edith and wishing I'd been a better friend to her. I felt bad that I'd been unable to get to her memorial service in Nantucket. Then, I fell asleep and had a dream…

"I was standing in a field when a great white owl floated down before me. It had the widest whitest wings and it had the most beautiful eyes," she recounted. "It just sat there on a branch a few feet away, looking at me."

"How did you feel when it looked at you?"

"So loved… it felt as if it was just projecting love at me."

"What do you think that was?"

"Oh, yes," she suddenly realized. "It was Edith!" Mom began to cry, but joyfully—with great relief. As we talked some more, my mother realized that the wise white bird had been beaming love to her to let her know that there was no reason to feel sad—that all was forgiven, that indeed, there had never been anything to forgive, for the friendship she'd shared with Edith was eternal.

A week later, Mom told me she'd started a painting of the white owl. She says that the dream "told her" to do this. It's a haunting and beautiful painting. It's also a healing.

Dreams for other people

Sometimes a friend or family member who's more open to receiving imagery will dream something for us. I've read stories in which dreamers receive information about the health of a friend or loved one; sharing this information has led to early detection of medical conditions—even saved lives!

One woman told me she'd dreamed of finding a piece of lost jewelry, a beautiful diamond bracelet, in the garden behind a bed of tulips.

"But I never had a bracelet like that," she said. "I didn't lose it." Still, the dream felt so important. Unable to understand it's meaning, she forgot about the dream until, about a week later, she met a woman at a party.

Though they'd never met before, they got to talking and then, the woman confided, "I've been so distracted lately. I lost a very special bracelet."

"What kind of bracelet?" the dreamer asked, chills up her spine.

"It was a family heirloom," the woman sighed. "A diamond bracelet."

Amazed, the dreamer shared the information she'd received. The next day, she received a phone call. "I found my bracelet—in the garden behind the tulips!"

Was the dreamer a psychic? Probably not. But she *was* open to receiving and trusting guidance and, knowing she'd be at the same party as the woman who'd lost the bracelet the angels had sent her the dream. They'd probably also guided the two women to talk to each other.

Why did they tell her and not the woman who had lost the bracelet?

The angels showed me:
*We offer help, guidance and support in
all situations but when you are afraid,
disoriented or in danger, we draw near,
doing all we can to keep you safe.*

FOURTEEN:

Protection

In a sense all angelic activity is protective but Heaven does seem
to have a soft spot for children, teenagers and the elderly. The angels
guide our children safely home when they wander. They warn them
away from accidents and help them (and us) through their tumul-
tuous teen years. Then, they help them with career, family life and
relationships. All the while, unseen hands catch people as they slip on
a patch of ice or fall from a ladder.

Perhaps the most compelling—and endearing—protective gesture I've read about (repeatedly) is the 'Angel Taxi.' Driven by a protective stranger, a taxi or other vehicle suddenly appears to help a
young person lost or stranded by car trouble or a missed connection
in a foreign country. Away from home and country, often for the first
time, with no cell phone connection, confused by maps and an un-
familiar language, kids can easily become disoriented and frightened.

Time and again, from down a deserted road or over a hill or
around a corner—a vehicle (a taxi, truck, or boat) appears. The driver,
who just happens to speak the same language—and as every story

reports, has the kindest eyes—offers to drive the lost kid directly to their destination—a youth hostel, hotel or vacation home, often free of charge. Then, as soon as safety is assured, the angel taxi disappears without a trace.

In one story, the mysterious (miraculous) cab driver was an American from the kid's own hometown! In another, a young woman reported, a bus pulled up beside her—on a road where no buses ran! She was the only passenger and the driver took her all the way home. It was only when she was safely inside that she realized, he'd never asked for her address but had known exactly where to take her!

The angels showed me:
The circle of love/light/life is eternal.
We have always been with you and we always
will be—from birth until death; and beyond.

FIFTEEN:

Messages from Loved Ones in Heaven

Your lost loved ones do not become angels. When people pass out of earthly life, they do not sprout wings or haloes. Our loved ones do not become birds or butterflies, either. But they can (and do) work with the angels to send us signs. The most commonly reported angel experiences *by far* are signs and messages received after the death of a loved one.

If you've experienced a such a sign, you know that they are deeply reassuring, loving and liberating. These signs release you from worry, letting you know that the people you've loved on Earth are happy and safe in Heaven—and helping you move on with your own life. From a call and response perspective, these signs are Heaven's *responses*, to your *call* for confirmation that life goes on.

The angels support grieving families at funerals and in the months that follow, sending butterflies, feathers, and other meaningful signs of undying love. They soothe loneliness, ease the grieving process and deliver solace to those left behind.

- A woman, grieving the death of her mother, hears a knock on her door. Opening it, she finds a strange woman. "I understand your mom just died," the stranger says. A rush of warmth floods the woman's body—she feels strangely peaceful, comforted and reassured. She thanks the stranger and closes the door behind her. But a moment later, she's flooded with questions. She wants to catch the woman, to ask her: Who are you? Where did you come from? How did you know about Mom? But, though it's been only a moment, the stranger has vanished.

- A woman tells me that after her husband's death, "Every night, I lie down in bed and raise my energy level and he lowers his and I feel him. He comes and he visits. He's protecting me, he's happy for me. I can feel a depression in the bed as if his body is there. But even without that, I can feel his presence next to me."

Read in the back seat

Typical signs from loved ones in Heaven may include:

- **'Pennies from Heaven':** We find a coin—not always a penny, and often many coins—in an unusual way or a surprising location (or both), hinting at a message from beyond.

- **Flowers:** Lilacs, roses and other flowering bushes that bloom in the middle of winter—almost always on the anniversary of an important or meaningful event. Flowers may also arrive in unusual ways. A stranger or a child may walk up and hand us a flower with a particular connection to the deceased; a TV show, radio program or sign may mention a meaningful flower just as we are asking for a sign. In fact, as people report, if there is a flower associated with the person we're missing, that flower will find its way to us.

- **Emails, phone messages:** A computer flashes a meaningful image from out of the blue and then returns to normal; a cell phone rings and the caller ID shows a deceased loved one's name (even when that person's cell phone has long since been disconnected).

- **Electrical phenomena:** Lights at home flash when someone mentions the loved ones name; the TV turns on or off by itself; lights that were turned off when we left a room go back on by themselves; car radios turn themselves on. These are just a few of the many electrical messages people report.

- **Music:** You hear 'your' song on the radio just after asking for a sign or thinking of someone; you are sitting in a café and suddenly, a song catches your ear and you gasp with recognition. You switch on the TV just as meaningful lines from a song are playing. Musical signs may come through dreams, through other people, through the media. If you get one, trust it!

- **Unusual encounters:** We find an object that reminds us of our deceased loved one in an unusual place. We encounter a stranger who reminds us of our loved one in manner or clothing, or even says something our loved one always used to say.

- **Dreams:** Many people receive dreams that communicate loving messages of comfort, reassurance that the loved one in Heaven is now happy. Dreams can even deliver important information. In one such dream, a brother transmitted the location of a missing document. In another, a grandfather pressed his daughter to phone her son, who was traveling in Europe. When she did, she discovered he'd been taken ill — and flew over to help him immediately.

Signs like these tell us: *I'm still here, loving and supporting you.*

They bring us closure, easing guilt about the things we didn't say or do, the visits or phone calls we forgot to make, the friendships we neglected.

Contact with our loved ones in Heaven is reassuring and deeply comforting.

It brings peace of mind to those left behind and brings closure to friends and family members who may not had the chance to say goodbye.

Dad's Homing Pigeon

When my father's brother David died, Dad hadn't seen him for a long time. In his last years, David, who lived in Florida, had developed Alzheimer's and my father, wrestling with his own health challenges, had moved into a nursing home in New York.

Dad was visibly shaken by the news. He didn't want to talk about it, and changed the subject to happier times.

About a week later, our family visited Dad on a beautiful spring morning. We were seated in a circle under a blossoming dogwood tree when Dad said, "There's this bird...

"I've been coming outside in the early morning and sitting out here by the river. There's no one else out yet, which is nice because the animals are more willing to communicate with me. I've been trying to get them to eat from my hand.

"But there's this one bird, a pigeon, that seems to have taken a special interest in me. It follows me, kind of hops along. It comes back, comes back. Funny little bird. Yesterday, it sat there so long that I asked it, 'What do you want?'

"I went inside and it went away. I thought that was the end of it.

But the next day, when I came out here, it was back. I can tell which one it is because all the other pigeons are that gray and blue color. This one's all white."

My sister, Beth, raised an eyebrow. Uncle David had loved birds, and flying. He'd grown up to become a decorated Air Force pilot—a fact of which Dad had spoken with pride. He'd also told us stories about their Bayside, Queens childhood—including the story of David's pigeons.

When David was 13 or 14 years old, he started raising homing pigeons on the roof. To get up there, he'd fashioned a rickety ladder, a set of steps precariously 'secured' between two planks of wood with a single nail on each end.

Dad, several years younger—and physically disabled—couldn't always use the dangerous ladder. But, he'd told us, "When all the steps were in, I went up on the roof with David.

One day, David saw a wild pigeon go by. "Watch this!" he told his little brother. Then, he opened his pigeon coop and released all of his birds. They went up and started flying around with the wild bird. A few minutes later, they brought it back. "The wild pigeon became part of the flock and David had another bird," Dad said.

So now, at the nursing home, Beth asked, "Dad, does the white pigeon remind you of anyone?"

"Should it?" he asked.

"Anyone you know have anything to do with pigeons?" I suggested.

My father's face lit with recognition. "Oh, David!" he said. "Wow!"

Since then, the white pigeon has stopped visiting Dad—another indication that it was sent to deliver a message. Once Dad received it, the bird disappeared. Still, I'm certain that if Dad starts missing David again, the bird will return—or another equally meaningful sign will arrive.

Experiences like this help us to understand and to trust that our loved ones are never "lost" to us and that our connection with them is always available. That's why, when you're sad or worried, you may receive a sign of comfort that whispers, "You are not alone."

If you need contact with a loved one in Heaven, ask for it.

Then, let it come in its own way and its own time. Let the signs the angels send bring you comfort. Your connection to your loved ones is eternal—in heaven as on earth.

The angels showed me:
No one dies alone.
At the time of transition, we
hover close, easing your passage and
comforting those who love you.

SIXTEEN:

Transition into light

When our time comes, no matter what we have done in the past, no matter our earthly regrets—the angels are with us. At all stages of life—and death—the angels' function is to support, encourage and bring us peace. They do not judge us—ever—for the things we may have done or not done. At the moment of death, the angels help ease our transition from physical to non-physical.

When people wrote to describe the death of a loved one, there were many correspondences in their accounts, most consistently:

- A calming energy: Described by one woman as, "a blanket of peace," this energy brings comfort to the dying and soothes witnesses.

- White light: Some people report seeing streams or beams of white light in the room—especially in the last moments of life and at the moment of transition.

- Orbs and clouds of light: Some people see 'orbs' (floating balls of light) or clouds of light in the corners of darkened rooms.

- Physical sensations: One woman described a "strong wave of energy" that moved through her own body as her mother passed.

- Luminous figures of light: Some report seeing glowing figures of light in corners of the room or over the bed.

- The dying may call out greetings—or sing along with music only they can hear. Witnesses report that when this light appears, even those who are in grave pain become peaceful, making an easier transition.

Goodbye messages

People who aren't present when a loved one passes may receive a 'goodbye' message—a mental image or gut feeling, a flash of knowing. "I just knew he was gone," they say.

For others, the goodbye message may be delivered as a phone call with no one on the line, the flashing of lights or a breeze of rose-scented air rushing through the room—delivered at the exact moment of death.

Grace Note: **About the Color White**

The angels often use the color white to signal their presence. Doctors and nurses in today's hospitals are free to wear colorful scrubs; however, when angel nurses make an appearance in a patient's room, they're often dressed in old-fashioned white uniforms—some even sport the starched white nurses' caps that today's nurses never wear.

When angels incarnate to rescue a stranded motorist, the cars, trucks and emergency vehicles they choose are often white—and often bear distinctive markings, license plates or words on a bumper sticker.

For example, when I was contemplating a job change, I was cut off in traffic by a white Nissan *Pathfinder*, with a sticker that read, *Go For It!* in the back window.

White objects and images may appear in dreams—and real life to signal the presence of angels. In Dad's story, the pigeon—unique among all the other birds in the area—was white. In the story of my mother's dream, the owl, signaling a message from Edith, was white. It's a kind of angel shorthand that we all, instinctively, understand.

V

Inviting the Divine

Inviting the Divine

An invitation is a gesture of welcome—an opening. A letter arrives in the mail, a hand is extended in friendship, a seat at the table is offered.

Come in. Sit down. Let's get to know each other.

Though you're already connected to the angels—always have been, always will be—this section is designed to invite you to see, feel and know that connection more fully.

The angels showed me:
Prayer is an invitation into a dynamic and
interactive 'call and response' relationship.
Your prayers are like ripples across the
Sea of Miracles. Our response echoes back
on a returning wave.

SEVENTEEN:

The Listening Universe

The purpose of the playing cards

I'd never told anyone—except my husband—about the playing cards. But I thought about them often. Why had the cards come to me? Why did it all feel so charged, even now? And why, every time I thought about it, did I feel so... stuck—as if there was something I was supposed to see or do?

I'd gotten married, had two children. I was a typical suburban stay-at-home mom driving carpools, picking up groceries, reading bedtime stories.

One day, more than ten years after the playing cards had come to me, I came to my journal to ask: *What did it mean? I still don't understand.*

I waited. I wanted to capture some deep truth—some glimmer of wisdom to share with others. I wanted everything to be tied up in a nice, neat bow of meaning.

Nothing happened.

I closed the book. I made tea. I came back to my desk. I stared out of the window. I waited. I opened the book. I scribbled some more thoughts—threads of ideas, to-do lists. I simply let come through my pen whatever needed to come.

Still, nothing happened.

Sighing, I closed the book again. That afternoon, I had some errands to run—a trip to the pharmacy and dry cleaners, a few phone calls. Just before it was time to pick up my children at school, I made a quick dash to the grocery store.

I pulled into the school parking lot just as the bell rang. I parked and stepped from the car, scanning the crowd for my children.

It was then that I looked down and saw, lying on the pavement beside my foot, a playing card, the *Two of Hearts.*

I stared at the card hopeless wonder. And all at once, I got it. Completely. Fully. And as I did, I started to laugh.

Everything that had happened, the coincidences, the synchronicities, the lost keys, the playing cards—all of it had been orchestrated to answer the one question I'd been asking for years: *God, are you there?*

And all of these years, in so many ways, the Universe had been responding: *Yes! I'm here—loving and supporting and guiding you, every step of the way.*

The Listening Universe

Before I started working with angel stories, if you'd asked, "Do you pray?" I'd have said no. When I look back, it's clear that, as I scribbled in my journals, I sensed a listener, hovering close enough to read what I'd written, and to respond.

I understand now that many people experience this sense of someone listening—and though many don't realize they're doing it, most people pray. From the *Please help*, whispered into silence in the middle of the night to the desperate, *Oh My God!* as a driver loses control of a car, we reflexively call out—to something, to *someone*. From the stories I've read, it's clear that these prayers are being answered—no matter how we pray, where we pray or even, to whom we pray.

I disagree

But it isn't just angels that come in response to our prayers. The angels are part of a much larger listening—a vast and interactive *listening universe* made by a profoundly generous Creator. The Sea of Miracles is a dynamic, shifting wholeness in constant flux; it expands and contracts, cycling into and out of form. It's a vast space-scape layered with galaxies and stars and is, at the same time, an organic, evolving, living and responsive consciousness.

This oceanic universe seems to have been designed intelligently, with great love, to respond to our needs, thoughts and prayers. Yet it was not designed *for* us—rather, at least, from my perspective, it is simply the nature of the Sea of Miracles to respond. *It is response.*

This universe is a living, generous protective sea—wrapped around all creation in a protective, supportive and integrated embrace—and though I know it may sound silly to say this, for me, the Universe is an enormous and comforting cosmic *hug*.

It calls to us, reaches toward us, magnetically, gravitationally as it reflexively, intrinsically (and often, messily) reacts and responds to our call and the calling that arises from all creation.

Every cell in your body, every fish in the sea, every star in the sky, all part of this breathing in (receiving) and breathing out (sending). And all of it designed to work together, to balance, to come to center. From our first grateful breath our every need is provided for—there is water to quench our thirst, sunlight to warm our skin, food springs up from the ground, all freely, abundantly provided.

This listening universe is designed to receive and respond to our every call. To imagine how it does this, think about the way that your cell phone works. Your cell phone is a receiver, programmed to scan constantly for incoming signals. When one of these signals, borne on invisible waves of light and sound, activates the phone, it *responds*—by ringing. In a similar way, your thoughts and prayers generate energy signals that pulse from you on invisible waves. These waves of consciousness cross the ocean of interconnected energy much as a pebble sends ripples pulsing across a pond.

They are met by a receiver—the part of the Sea of Miracles best suited to answer. Then, in an answering wave, the response bounces back to you, as answered prayer. When we experience a flash of intuition, or receive a sign, synchronicity or message it has been sent to us across this interconnected "sea". That flash, chance meeting or message is guidance.

The house we did not buy

We'd been looking for years, renting a house "until we find something we like." But after ten years of renting, I'd pretty much given up on that dream. Then, I found it—a little gem of a cottage on a quiet street—walking distance from town, two blocks from the river.

When my husband loved it too and our offer was accepted, I was over-the-moon ecstatic. But now, just two weeks from the closing date, all the joy had drained away. I felt desperate—and so did my husband.

With the stress of making so many big financial decisions at once, we'd fallen back into our old patterns of blaming and bickering. And one afternoon, after another argument, I called my spiritual counselor in tears.

Heart breaking, I cried for my husband who worked so hard, for myself, for the long-awaited dream home that seemed to be dissolving before my eyes.

"I can't do this anymore," I said. "If buying this house means living in a war zone, I don't want it."

My counselor suggested I take a drive, sit in a café and think things through with my journal and a cup of tea.

I got into the car. I'd already cried until there was no sadness left. Now, as I drove my eyes continued to stream tears as if some inner sponge was being squeezed, releasing a deep, wet saltiness.

About a block away from the café, it occurred to me to pray.

God, I asked silently, *please take this situation and work it out so that everyone can be happy. Help us to make this choice in freedom, towards love.*

One moment later, a white car cut in front of me. Hitting my brakes to avoid it, I stared at its license plate, which displayed a few letters and the numbers: *444.*

I knew that angel signs are often delivered by white vehicles — plus I'd *just* written a story about angel numbers, quoting Doreen Virtue: *Seeing 4's? The angels are with you!* And I laughed, amused by the playfulness of the message, and that shifted my focus away from my pain so I could receive it. *We're here,* the angels had let me know. *Right in front of you, the moment you need us.*

Feeling better, I took my seat at a favorite table, opened my journal and began to write. I let it all out, writing furiously at first, then, more calmly, more thoughtfully.

Suddenly, I looked up.

Everything in the restaurant had fallen silent. It was as if someone had thrown a switch and a curtain of sound — the espresso machine, the piped in music, the people talking, the baby crying — had suddenly, strangely parted. At the same time, everything seemed slowed down, dreamlike.

Then, a man on the other side of the room leaned over to whisper to his wife and somehow, in that strange silence, I heard him. "Four-forty-four?" he asked her.

"Yes," she confirmed. "Four-forty-four."

A moment later, the café burst back to life—cappuccino machine roaring a froth of sound, cash register drawers clicking open and shut, classical guitar music filling the air.

Stunned, I watched as the couple stood to leave. As he held her coat and she shrugged into it, a gesture they'd practiced for years, I thought of my own husband—our years together and my eyes brimmed once again.

Suddenly, my cell phone rang.

"I'm sorry," my husband said. "We can work this out. I love you."

"I love you, too," I said, and as the mysterious couple exited the café, my heart filled with light.

That would have been enough. But it didn't end there.

A few minutes later, I drove to the high school where I was helping with the costumes for the school play. As I entered, two dads were standing in the hallway drinking coffee from white Styrofoam cups and discussing a football game.

"What's the score?" one man asked the other.

The other man pulled out his Blackberry to check. "Four—forty-four," he reported.

"Okay, I get it!" I whispered out loud, as I walked by. Laughing I thought of the angels, fluttering along behind me, amusing me with their multiple messages.

Backstage, I joined the other volunteer moms around a table piled with costumes—satin ball gowns, tulle-skirted tutus, and velvet jackets. "Here," someone said, handing me a pink and green ballerina costume with a split seam.

Let yourself dance, I remembered. Another sign? I smiled again.

I began stitching. As I sewed each stitch became a metaphor for the way that life delivers lessons: One stitch at a time our lessons line up before us, slowly, steadily so we can learn them — it's an endless tapestry, endlessly sewn.

"Excuse me," a voice interrupted my reverie.

A 16-year-old boy with huge blue eyes and long black hair stood before me. Dressed in full costume, a brown leather tunic over green leggings, his striking features (and my state of mind) made him appear (for a moment) as an ancient hunter, just stopping to see me before returning to his home among the trees and wild animals.

"I found this," he said, and then, he handed me a bright purple feather.

And here I have to stop and say that, I *knew* the feather had fallen from a costume, probably one of the elaborate masks the players would wear on the stage. But I knew, also, that this was a sign. For this young man could have handed the feather to any of the dozen women in that room and that feather could have been any color — but all of it had been orchestrated by the angels to deliver a final sign so power-packed, so specific and personal that I couldn't — even if I'd tried — deny it.

A *feather,* the angels signature sign to me, in *purple,* the color of highest spiritual resonance, the color of Archangel Michael, my closest guide. I was overcome with awe — and with the sense of being loved more deeply than I could even fathom — so deeply that the angels would do all of this, just to ease my bruised heart.

I took the feather and I thanked my young messenger, and as he turned away, I called, "Wait. What's your name?"

He turned back, grinning. "Freedom," he answered.

God bless his hippie parents, his *name* was Freedom!

∞

I want you to notice a couple of things about this story. First, look at the prayer that I made. I didn't ask, *Please make Matthew agree with me* or, even, *Please make the house cost less.* I said a *soul prayer.* I asked for the thing I truly desired—freedom from the cycle of arguing and the sadness it caused in me, and a home filled with peace, and love.

Second, notice that the response came through little signs—a license plate, an overheard conversation, a feather—yet created huge and powerful waves. *You are not alone,* it told me. *You are loved—by the angels, and the people in your life.*

This message was the beginning of a powerful wave of healing, flooding my whole life with light.

So, even though we didn't buy that house, we moved fully into the house we already had. For the first time in our 25-year marriage, my husband and I began to think of —and to treat—each other as partners. We made the house where we already lived more comfortable, more beautiful—with paint, rearranged furniture and a deep cleaning.

But the real shift went much deeper. We began to see the patterns that had kept us wounded and separate in the past; the scars that blocked us from loving each other. Together, we uncovered and began to work our way through them. Together, finally, we built a house filled with love.

The angels showed me:
*We see all aspects of all situations. Give us
your worries and concerns and allow us to
resolve them in a way that uplifts and brings
peace to everyone involved.*

EIGHTEEN:

Soul Prayer

In the story in the previous chapter—The house we did not buy—I said a soul prayer—a way of praying which, the angels have shown me is particularly powerful. Soul prayer releases the 'how' of the situation to the angels' wisdom. Instead of praying for a particular outcome—*Please make John love me; please don't let Patrick die,* we acknowledge that we have no authority over the lives or choices of others. We surrender our worry, our need to control the exact way things will work out to Divine order, asking that *the situation resolve itself for the greatest good for all involved.*

In this way, you may not receive the exact result for which you pray—the life may not be saved, the house may be lost forever; the relationship may not work out as you'd hoped it would. But something else will come. The angels are able to deliver an outcome more amazing and delightful than anything you could imagine.

Trusting that the Universe was designed to respond to your call—and that the angels have your welfare in mind—you say a soul prayer: *Bring me peace with what comes, and until it comes, peace with what is.* You say it in full faith that things can and will get better.

Working with Soul Prayer

Instead of asking for a certain person to love you, ask:
Please increase my experience of love itself; bring more love into my life; bring to me the people, and experiences, that will open my heart.

Instead of praying for a specific job, ask:
Please bring to me the opportunities where I can use my unique gifts and talents; lead me to the situations and experiences that encourage me to be of service while also receiving the money and resources I need to be happy.

Instead of asking for money:
Ask for the outcome that you hope that having the money would bring by asking: *Please resolve this situation in the best way for all involved.* Now, instead of delivering cash, the angels may deliver household appliances, dissolve old debts, and coordinate situations that we, from our limited perspective could not have dreamed of.

Instead of asking: *Why is this happening to me?*
Try a soul prayer: *Take this problem/situation/mess from me <u>now</u>. Guide me to the choices and actions that will improve my situation. I am being guided to the choices and actions that will lead me into the light.*

Instead of asking: *Why can't I ever catch a break?*
Try a soul prayer: *Open new opportunities for me <u>now</u>. Guide me to the people and situations that can best utilize, support and appreciate the gifts I have to offer. I know that from now on, every choice I make is an opportunity to change my life for the better.*

Instead of asking: *Why is my life so messed up?*
Try a soul prayer: *Clear the negative energy from my life, from my thoughts and emotions <u>now</u>. I release this situation to your hands, knowing*

that you, who can do anything, can easily untangle this situation, delivering an outcome that serves the highest good for all involved.

Instead of asking: *Why don't my relationships work out?*
Try a soul prayer: *Guide me <u>now</u> to the people and situations that resonate with and bring out my greatest joy and self-expression. Guide me to the people who love me as I am.*

Finally, be gentle with yourself.

Give yourself time to shift from old patterns of thinking and praying. You've been practicing those patterns for a long time. So it may take a bit of repetition to set a new thought/prayer permanently into place. Simply adjust, ask again and let it go.

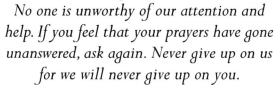

The angels showed me:
No one is unworthy of our attention and help. If you feel that your prayers have gone unanswered, ask again. Never give up on us for we will never give up on you.

NINETEEN

The Matter of Unanswered Prayers

When someone asks me, "Why can't I receive, feel or sense my angels' guidance? Why don't they answer my prayers?" I tell them... "I don't know."

It's easy to blame yourself—to think that if only you did more good, or worked harder, or prayed in a different way, God would hear you. But my experience tells me this kind of thinking is misguided.

I know that from inside a crisis it can seem as if you're completely alone in the world. I know that hearing some cheerful Pollyanna say, "God loves you," does little to reassure you. When you're wrestling with despair or challenged by a crisis, you know exactly what you want. *Make it stop! Take the pain away! Bring my dear one back to me!*

The misunderstanding arises from our belief:
- That we can control how, when—and if—our prayers will be answered.
- That, unless God sends the angels swooping in to fix our life, there is something wrong with us—or with God.

But these things are simply not true. There are things the angels simply cannot and will not do. They can't bring the dead back to life. They won't manipulate another person into being or doing anything just to make you happy. They can't change the fact that eventually, all of us will die.

But there are ways to draw the angels closer, to ask for and receive signs of comfort and the reassurance that you're not alone.

1) **Ask for help.** It may surprise you to know that even in their darkest hour, many people are reluctant to call on the angels — especially if they feel as if their prayers have been ignored. But the angels cannot answer a question that hasn't been asked. Don't be shy with the angels and don't hide your need. No request is too big or too small. Don't hide your hurt — or your heart. The angels never judge us. They understand and welcome your expressions of emotion, your tears. They don't care if you get angry. Their only concern is to bring you peace.

2) **Ask for signs** — that your prayers have been heard and the angels are with you. These signs are often all we need to shift into a different energy — a different frame of mind — out of which we can begin to act on our own behalf. Signs also open us to the possibility that the angels' help may come in unexpected ways.

3) **Relax your ideas about how guidance 'should' work.** Are you asking for a specific result and missing guidance that may be coming in some other way? The most common story I hear is, "I was asking for a specific sign — a dream, a butterfly or a particular song — and missing the guidance that was coming all along in another way." (Most often through intuition, feelings or mental images.)

4) **Recognize the response that does come.** We may not always realize that our prayer has been answered—or we may refuse to acknowledge the answer that comes. We may be confused. "I don't understand this, I asked for someone to love and I got a call from a head hunter?" Or, "I asked to be guided to the perfect job and nothing happened… oh, except I got this invitation to a party…" As the angels have shown me, again and again, when I follow their guidance (even when it doesn't seem to make sense) things work out in the most remarkable ways.

5) **Work your prayers.** Often, the angels don't fix a problem for us but rather, send intuitive guidance about actions we can take to fix it ourselves. They may even send other people to help us. Sometimes, this guidance asks us to step out of our comfort zone—to change a habit or try something new.

Examples include: praying for healing and missing intuitive nudges to change the lifestyle habits that are causing the illness; praying for a new job but ignoring your soul's promptings to take up a new career or to reach out to an old colleague; praying for a soul mate but ignoring your sudden interest in a class at the conference center; praying for money but refusing offers of charity or help from other people out of pride.

For me, unanswered prayers are always about my own reluctance and resistance to act. I ask for a slimmer body but I don't want to go to the gym. I want the angels to follow me with a cosmic liposuction device, gently siphoning off the extra pounds in my thighs. But even if the angels could do that for me—and I sincerely believe they can—I still need to work my prayers. So, I follow the guidance the angels send—and often, that guidance sends me to yoga or on a long walk through the farm across the street from my home. The angels

angels

offer guidance about healthy foods to eat—even what time to go to sleep. When you 'work your prayers' the angels' guidance works.

Help the angels help you:
1) Do all you can to attune to resonance with the Divine.
2) Follow the guidance that comes.
3) Build a case for Grace. Become a Grace detective. Seek out stories in books and other media about real people who've experienced the touch of the Divine. Ask friends if they've ever experienced such things. Look for patterns in the stories. How did it happen? What are the stages of a divine encounter? How does Grace work? By seeking out and following such stories, you immediately begin to attune to Divine energy.

I know because I've witnessed it: When you take even the smallest step toward Grace, a whisper in the dark, a scribble on the back of a napkin, Grace will rush to meet you.

Cultivate Wonder
Let the Divine Look Through Your Eyes

Abraham Henschel once wrote, "Awareness of the Divine begins with wonder." Awareness begins, also, with presence. For we must be present in order to experience the wonder right before our eyes.

To cultivate this awareness, this wonder, this presence, try this:

All day, let your consciousness recede one step backwards and invite Divine awareness to step forward. Let it look through your eyes.

What shifts?

Try it while looking out the window.

What does the Divine make of that snowy scene? What does that sky, crowded with puffy clouds look like through the eyes of the Divine?

Try it while sitting in traffic; in the office; at home.

What catches the attention? What falls away? What details leap up, what colors, what textures?

Let Divine awareness fill your body—let it feel with your senses. How does it respond when it sees that color or that person across the room?

Try it right now. Look up. What's here?

As I write this, the waitress keeps walking up and chattering to me, distracting me, breaking my concentration.

At first I am frustrated and upset. Does this mean I will no longer be able to work here? I think. I love this restaurant. Will she ruin everything? Then, I laugh. Here is the perfect opportunity to practice the very thing I'm writing about.

I let the Divine look through my eyes at her and I see her wide-open face, her childlike, welcoming heart, inviting me to play, to connect, to converse. She is not bothering me, she is reaching out and I, distracted by all my lofty ideas, am distracted and distant. In my attempt to teach presence, I am the one who is removed from the present moment while she, Puckish, is inviting me back into the moment where real life is being lived.

Thanks to that invitation, I am flooded with sensation. I hear the music, a sweet, high-pitched song with flute and piano and a strange, high-pitched whistle. Thanks to her 'interruptions' I hear the words—about love and listening. I notice the fans gently turning the air, the water dripping from the ice where the oysters are stored.

The Divine is not interested in my theories. It is interested in my fingers, touching the keys, the gold ring on my finger—a symbol of 30 years of love. The Divine, it seems, is interested in everything and anything—the snow heaped in the parking lot, the light through the bottles—green, gold, red jewels—lined up above the bar.

I see that, when I let the Divine look through my senses, it is interested in the details that make the world what it is—this white china teacup, this little pitcher of cream, the smoky rich taste of this imported tea, the white salt crystals, the pebbly grey and black crushed pepper in their glass shakers.

In a Divine paradox, awareness does not happen only in meditation, on yoga retreat or in prayer. True awareness happens here—in the nitty gritty of the world. This table, that snowscape, this waitress.

Extra Credit: In the presence of a person or situation with which you are in conflict, let the Divine step forward. See it through the eyes of that presence, that awareness: unconditional, curious, intrigued and open. Not judging. Just present to what is here.

VI

Calling/Response

—

Your Glowing Chip of Moonlight

The entrance door to the sanctuary is inside of you.

-Rumi

The angels showed me:
*You have a divinely given task: To live your life
as fully as you can; to penetrate your fascinations
as deeply as you can; to love as completely as you
can. Our task is to support, guide and help you,
to bring you peace, as you find your way.*

TWENTY:

Call and Response

When I finally understood the meaning of my playing cards experience, something deep and fierce clicked into place. I AM A WRITER. This felt like a revelation, sudden and surprising. Yet it felt, at the same time, inevitable—as if a veil had been pulled back revealing something that had been there all along.

I'd *always* been a writer. It was there in early childhood when my mother read to me and my sisters from the picture books she'd written and illustrated herself; it was there in my early interest in reading. In fact, my first memory of deep joy is the day when my mother took me to the library where I discovered that there was a whole world of books—I can still remember sitting at the center of the children's section, surrounded by towers of books—and discovering that I could take them home, as many as I wanted!

You've had experiences like this yourself, times when your heart leapt, when you worked for hours, completely immersed in a task, that moment when you felt inexplicably drawn to something. This is calling. The convergence of what you love and that which is constantly loving that part of you into being.

My calling to be a writer bursts from the journals stacked in my bedroom closet; it was there when my high school English teacher introduced me to poetry by playing "The Dangling Conversation", a Simon and Garfunkel song. It was there when I first understood that authors embed hidden symbols in their stories—when I realized that filmmakers were doing the same thing.

All of my life, the stories I found in books were my teachers, my friends, my constant and steady companions yet it had never occurred to me that this thing that I loved to do, that I did as naturally as breathing would turn out to be my life's work, *my calling.*

I thought it was supposed to be more complicated. This was too easy.

As I shifted from imagining I might someday become a writer to actually being one, opportunities seemed to materialize out of thin air. When a press release I'd written for a volunteer organization was sent to a local newspaper, the editor called. "Who wrote this?" she asked. She offered me a writing job—a monthly parenting column.

You can imagine the thrill of seeing my name in print—and being paid to do what I loved most! As always happens when we are on the right path, doors swung open and I was led to coincidental meetings with editors—one, at a hotel swimming pool, of all places, where my son befriended a little girl who turned out to be the child of the editor of a top parenting magazine!

One thing led to another. I got bigger assignments—more experience, more confidence. By now, my husband was pushing me to try an editorial job. "You love magazines," he said, pragmatically. "Why not work at one of them?" But, I'll never get a job like that, I argued.

Try, **a little voice urged.**

Oh, why not, I smiled. I'd learned to write down my goals when I was in the DMA office. I'd learned that doing so makes them more focused, more real.

That day, I penned the intention in my journal: *I work for a (real) magazine,* adding a list of all the things I wanted from the job: Flexibility to be with my children, work that helped women, children and families, something meaningful to do. Oh yes, I also wanted to travel.

A day or two later, I was in a café when an abandoned newspaper caught my eye. It wasn't a paper I normally read. But there was something about it...

I picked it up and randomly flipped through it while sipping my tea. There, in the middle of the page, lay a small, three-line ad. *Editor.* There was nothing special about the ad, no color, nothing to make it stand out from the other advertisements on the page. Yet, to me, it seemed to glow right off the page.

Wow! I was intrigued. But then, I have no experience, I thought, setting the paper aside. I had something to eat. I read the novel I'd brought along.

Then, *Write down the phone number.* **The little voice had returned.**

But I...

Try. Heart quickening, I wrote down the phone number on a little scrap of paper. I put it in my pocket and tried, unsuccessfully, to misplace it several times. But it kept floating up.

Finally, I made the call.

A week later, when the Features Director called to tell me, "You're hired," I was stunned. It had happened so fast—it had been so easy that when I hung up, my whole body was shaking.

Three days later, I was sobbing: *I can't start work next week — I have nothing to wear!*

I'd tried on every work-appropriate garment I owned but, though my closet was filled with beautiful designer clothes — suits and blouses and shoes — after having two babies, those size-6 skirts no longer fit my size-12 body. The shoes — delicate size 5 heels and strappy sandals — were useless on my pregnancy-swollen, two-sizes-larger feet.

We didn't have the money for new clothes — honestly, we didn't have the money for food! But I couldn't show up at the office in my Mommy costume — sweats and stretched out tee shirts. I can still remember sitting on the floor in my bedroom, holding one of my beautiful brown shoes — a Joan and David pump — tears dripping from my chin, and pleading: *Please help me!*

About an hour later…

I was sitting on the sofa, reading to my children from a picture book when my husband came in, carrying a bag of trash.

"I found this on the curb," he explained. "Is it yours?"

"Mine?"

He'd found the bag where we'd normally place the cans on pick-up day. Thinking I'd mistakenly put the trash out early, he'd picked it up, planning to carry it back to the porch. But it didn't feel like trash and, pulling the bag open to peek…

We poured out the contents of the bag on the living room floor and stared, amazed. There were two brand new designer suits (one navy blue, one brown), a black wool blazer, and two silk blouses — all in my new bigger size. There were a couple of silk scarves and a hand-bag. Best of all, three pair of *new* size 7 shoes, perfect for the office!

Incredible? Impossible?

Let me assure you, it happened—and the same kinds of things will happen to you. In fact, they are already happening. I promise.

God has been sending the angels to answer your prayers all of your life.

Sometimes you sense this. Sometimes you lose touch with the guidance that's streaming toward you and you may feel lost and alone. But the guidance hasn't gone away and the bridge to connection is always there. All you have to do is remove the veils that block you from seeing and knowing who you really are: a blessed and beloved child of the Universe with a constant and eternal connection to the Divine.

The angels showed me:
You don't need to hide your light, beauty
and joy under veils of scar tissue anymore.
A universe of love lives within you, waiting
to be born through you. Let yourself open to
our love. Let your life shine.

TWENTY-ONE:

Your Glowing Chip of Moonlight

Virtually every prophet, spiritual teacher, philosopher and poet from antiquity to present time has described our everyday world of matter and forms—a world which seems so real—as a veil, concealing a deeper, more 'real' world. This veiling, they teach, is essential, for it protects us from that which, if revealed all at once, would overwhelm us.

Just as we are cautioned not to look directly at the face of God, so the Divine reveals itself to us gradually, slowly, over a lifetime, veil by delicate veil. This endless unfolding of revelation and beauty captivates and intrigues us, leading us forward and, ultimately, inward.

In one of the great paradoxes of the spiritual path, we come to a moment when we realize: The more I search, the more I am led back to myself, a radiant free being with a meaningful purpose and a direct personal connection with the Divine. This being lives at the center of your heart—a core self, unchanging, containing the pattern of who you really are. I call this core self the *I Am.*

The *I Am*

The *I Am* lives in the heart—not in the mind. It's not logical, not rational. Neither is it irrational. The *I Am* uses a completely different kind of reasoning than the mind—a soul logic, out of which it makes choices that 'feel' right. When we are in touch with the *I Am* we are not figuring things out. Instead, we are feeling our way. You might say that when we are in touch with the *I Am* we are thinking with the heart.

Like the "glowing chip of moonlight" I described in Chapter Two, the *I Am* is always present, illuminating the deep cavern of the self, no matter what. Even when things feel like they're spinning out of control, still the *I Am* is there, solid, strong, constant. It's a deep well of peace—a glowing chip of the Divine.

The *I Am* is a refuge, a haven, an oasis of deep sanctuary —and you don't have to travel to find it. It is right inside of you.

The *I Am* contains your *soul seed,* the psychic DNA of your unique intention, your life gesture, the reason you decided to come forth and be born. The *I Am* knows what you came to Earth to accomplish, even if you are not consciously aware of this mission.

When I'm working with a client, the *I Am* shines out like the sun. It's the liquid/solid golden core of self—like melted gold—that flows through and around the realm of the heart. At other times, it appears solid, a living organ made of soul tissue that links us directly to the Divine—a flowing, living bridge between you and God.

Hmmm? You may be saying. That sounds just like Amy's description of the angels: Pure white light, made of love, a bridge,

a connection to God.

That's because the *I Am* is just like an angel—an angel that formed at the moment the consciousness that would become *you,* decided to be born—with the same intention all angels share, to guide you toward peace.

Some people might call the *I Am* the *Soul.* That name is fine, too. I needed to rename it, because for me, the word soul had become confused. You can call it anything you want: The Soul, the Core Self, the Higher Self. The name is not important. Simply tune into your own heart and find the name that resonates for you.

When you are in touch with your *I Am,* you begin to see and to treat yourself as the angels would treat you.

From this perspective, you understand that you are a precious part of the whole, a holographic gem in Indra's interconnected net. From this perspective, you see past personality, past your history or your mistakes. From the point of view of the *I Am,* you realize: *I am Light. I am Love. I am Life.*

Or as God is reported to have stated it: *I Am That I am.* This is a powerful mystical statement, one that has been studied for centuries by the learned sages of all modern faith paths. For me, it is a confirmation of what the angels showed me: all things and beings are of God and all things and beings contain God as God contains all things, and all of it resonates with the same love, light, life energy —the "I am" of awareness, of Shekinah, of Christ Consciousness.

You've heard it said that you were created in the image of the Divine. Here's what that means to me.

It means that you, too, are light, are love, are life, expressing itself. You, too, are expansive, generous, loving and supportive. You, too, are beautiful and meant to shine. You, too, are whole, and out of that wholeness, you are generative, creative and juicy, bursting with life.

This awareness is the gift of the *I Am*. As you deepen your connection with the *I Am*, you naturally align with the angels. You begin to make *higher choices*.

You begin to treat others as the angels would treat them.

Your heart opens to your spouse, your children, your parents. So when your kid messes up, you don't shout, you *reach* out. You teach him, through the example of your kindness and support, that he is loved no matter what he does — just the way the angels love him (and you).

Your heart opens to strangers, making them seem less strange.

When a waitress makes a mistake, you don't berate her, you *help* her. You reassure her that we all make mistakes, that everyone has a bad day now and then. You treat her with the same tenderness and support with which the angels treat you. You see her as she really is — through the eyes of love, for those are the eyes of the *I Am*.

Your heart opens to yourself, deepening your integrity and self-esteem.

When you are supposed to be somewhere, you show up on time and prepared. When the clerk at the supermarket undercharges you, you *tell her*. You do your best at work. You don't cut corners. When you don't understand something, you ask. At the same time, when you make a mistake, you forgive yourself.

Locating the *I Am*

When you first begin to feel around for the *I Am*, you will naturally gravitate first to things that are *not* the *I Am*.

- Roles and descriptions like: I'm a mom; I'm nice; I'm a little overweight; I'm a great cook.
- Positions you hold in your community like: I'm a church leader; a manager; a married man.
- Qualities and characteristics: I'm organized. I'm shy. I'm kinda depressed.

These things are not the *I Am*, nor are so-called 'spiritual' qualities like: I'm intuitive; I teach yoga; I'm a Reiki Master; I'm a healer. Though each of these may be an expression of the *I Am*, the *I Am* is not a role, not a label or identity. It's not your personality or your ego; it's completely different—and infinitely broader, wider than any of these. The *I Am* is a *field*—a unique psychospiritual DNA that forms the core self, you, in its purest state, without the earthly roles or masks of personality.

Thoughts like, *"I'm a mother"* or *"I run a million dollar company"* are ideas about ways you may express yourself through work or the activity of raising a family. But these things are not who you are. They are like clothing that you put on and later, take off. They are like cars that you drive for a while and then, later, trade in for new cars.

You are so much more than these things.

In the same way that white light contains all of the colors of the rainbow, so your *I Am* is a spectrum, containing all the many shades of you. As a prism can break white light into all of its colors, your human life gives you the chance to express yourself in many different ways. As a rainbow is a visible expression of all the colors of white light, so your life is a multi-layered, multi-colored expression of the resonant core of *you*.

As I write this book, I am an author, a mother, a teacher, a customer of the café where I sit, a driver of the car that brought me here.

I am all of these things—and none of them, for if these roles, activities and expressions were stripped away, the *I Am* would still remain.

The *I Am* helps me align all of these things into a congruent, holistic *life gesture*—a way of living that is aligned with the Divine while also aligned with my reason for being here, the mission and purpose for which I was born.

It aligns these things in the same way the Universe takes the people and animals and fish and birds and plants and insects and trees and grasses and sorts it all together, finding a place for every single one.

As you acknowledge:
- "It is true that I love being a mother. But that is only one expression of what I truly am."
- "It is true that I work as a doctor. But that is only one expression of what I truly am."
- "It is true that I am currently a student. But that is only one expression of what I truly am."

You naturally wonder...
- What then, am I?
- What is the essential me?
- What, when all of these roles and jobs are stripped away, is left?

When you ask, the answer comes. I am ...
- Light, expressing itself through these thoughts, these ideas, these creative impulses.
- I am Love, expressing itself through these feelings, these drives and emotions.

- I am Life, expressing itself through this breath, these actions, this body, these movements.
- Suddenly, the truth is revealed: I am an expression of the light, love, life energy of All That Is.

Meditation:
Meeting/Revealing the *I Am*

We cannot understand the *I Am* with the intellect. The only way to experience it is with the heart. We begin by clearing a space where the *I Am* can reveal itself.

Sit quietly and close your eyes. Take a few deep breaths and relax.

Now, imagine that you are sitting in a wide and clear room completely flooded with white light. Imagine, also, that this room is flooded with love and with welcome. This is the room of the Divine. Now imagine that this room that you are sitting in is also resting in you—at the center of your heart. See this room there, in you, flooded with light. See if you can hold the two ideas, which seem to be mutually exclusive, in your thoughts at the same time. I am sitting in the room of the Divine. At the same time, the room of the Divine rests within me. Flip back and forth, shifting from within the room back to the room within you.

Now, imagine that this room is also the room where the Divine waits patiently, eternally holding its heart space open just for you.

This heart space, described by mystics of all faiths, has been imagined in many ways: As a castle, a bridge, a pathway of light. But this is your room—your space. How does it feel to you?

Like a cave with adobe red walls? An outdoor clearing in the middle of a forest? A breeze-swept room overlooking the ocean?

There's no right or wrong picture. Drop into your own heart and let yourself see and know.

Turn your attention to your breathing, just following the in and out of your breath. Inhale and as you exhale, ask yourself: Who's breathing? Who am I? Notice what answer comes. If what arises is a job or a role you play, that is not the I Am. Look deeper. Who is meeting the Divine? Who is observing this meeting? Now open your eyes.

For extra credit, when you face a challenge, a question, or a crisis, ask: What would the *I Am* do here? Listen for an answer. When it comes, acknowledge that this answer is guidance. Consider following it.

VII

The Parallel Path

–

Invitation from the Angels

Nothing may be truly said to be a 'miracle' except in the profound sense that everything is a miracle.

\- Paramahansa Yogananda

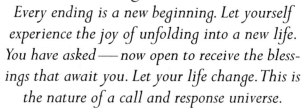

The angels showed me:
*Every ending is a new beginning. Let yourself
experience the joy of unfolding into a new life.
You have asked — now open to receive the blessings that await you. Let your life change. This is
the nature of a call and response universe.*

TWENTY-TWO:

The Parallel Path

It was the end of my son's senior year of high school. In just a
few months, he would graduate. A few months later, he'd be gone.
Though I'd been anticipating this transition for over a year, I was
overwhelmed with loss. *Make it stop,* I prayed, wandering the house
in a fog of grief. *This is the most exciting time of his life. I should be
celebrating with him.*

One morning, as I was coming up the stairs, I found a birds' nest
tucked into the gap between the air conditioner and the frame of the
window.

At any other time of day, I'd have missed it — but at that hour,
with the sun angled just so, I was able to see, silhouetted against the
plastic air-conditioner sleeve, the heads of three tiny birds. Moving
closer, I heard them rustling about, softly peeping.

Suddenly the mother bird arrived and pushed into the nest with
a great flapping. Mesmerized, I crouched low to watch. As she fed
her hatchlings, I was reminded of my own early days of mother-
ing — the endless hours, the flying about, the way that, burning with

lack of sleep and frustration, I'd longed for this day, when my children would be grown and I'd have time...

Time for what? The question swam up from deep inside. *What will you be able to do now, that you could not do while raising your 'birds'?* I thought about the books I could now write, the trips I could take, and a wave of eagerness swept through me. In the coming days, I began to let go. I turned my attention from loss and endings toward beginnings and, in so doing, toward hope.

A week later, I sat in the crowded school gym and I celebrated my son's accomplishment and mine. When the ceremony was over, I hugged him with pure joy—and pride. I'd been a good mother. My son was ready for the next part of his journey, and I was ready for mine.

I drove home in deep contemplation. A gentle rain was falling, my windshield wipers rhythmically sweeping the windshield. Suddenly, as I was moving beneath an overpass, something dropped from the steel girders above, becoming entangled in my windshield wipers. Startled, I pulled to the side of the road.

It was some kind of debris, I thought, as I got it free but ...

It's a birds' nest! I realized. I examined the fragile weaving of twigs, feathers and the paper strip from a Hershey's Kiss and suddenly, my heart overflowed with gratitude. With tears in my eyes, I set the precious gift on the seat beside me and drove home.

∞

The angels showed me:
*Everything in the universe reaches
for expansion, eternally unfolding into
light, becoming more.*

The Light, Love, Life That Calls to You

Are there really angels? Of course. Can I prove this? Not yet—though the thousands of stories I've read build a strong case that something is going on. From my perspective, it seems as if angels are appearing more often, to more people than ever before. Is this true? How could we possibly know?

Still, there are some things we can measure—some things of which I am certain. When I ask for help, help comes and, in a kind of Divine alchemy, when I live as if the world is a Sea of Miracles, it becomes just that: My body heals, my relationships transform, opportunities present themselves, problems become gifts.

This will happen for you.

You have established connection with the chip of Divine light that glows at the center of your heart. You have seen that the Divine is in everything. You have peeked behind the curtain of your own

141

astonishing beauty, even if you've only been able to do so for a moment.

Your life will never be the same.

For when you connect with the energy of the Divine, you open to a stream of signs, synchronicity and miracles. Your cares lighten, your problems ease. You begin to experience a kind of inner *spaciousness*, a feeling of quiet, restful alertness, and you may experience flashes of acute awareness, sensing the presence of who you are beyond form.

Chances are, you will notice this first while doing something that allows the chatter of your mind to quiet—something like driving or washing the dishes or sitting in the back yard and watching the sun set behind the house next door. This sudden momentary glimpse behind the curtain will intrigue and perhaps, move you, activating a sense of wonder and curiosity.

Cultivating this peaceful, mindful state of *presence* will increase your ability to see and to receive symbolic and intuitive guidance.

You can do this by walking out-of-doors, without cell phone or music player, simply holding yourself in a state of relaxed and expectant listening or by doing the exercises in this book. You might choose to take up a practice of meditation, yoga or tai chi or even, a meditative activity like knitting or listening to instrumental music.

One day, you may experience *flow*, the psycho-spiritual state in which you feel positive, energized, focused and alive. This *flow state* is available in all parts of your life but most people experience it first, through deep concentration while doing creative work or fully engaging in physical activity or through meditation.

You will seek out the people with whom you can really be yourself and the places where people like you are gathering. This is a natural phase of spiritual unfolding, the search for the soul's true community.

As you connect with your true self, old interests will reemerge, and dreams that you once cherished—as a child or young adult—will bubble up to fill your life with new energy and new meaning. What joy you will feel as, one by one, you open the closets of your soul and reveal these once hidden selves—the creativity, talents and interests that were always there, were always you.

As Divine light streams into your life, people will notice.

"You look different," they'll say, and you'll know just what they mean because you feel different—lighter, with more energy and enthusiasm. As you lose tolerance for stale or toxic relationships, mind-numbing activities and inane entertainments, they will fall easily away and more nourishing and empowering friendships and interests will bloom.

You will develop a *mountaintop perspective*.

One day, you will lift up from the story of your suffering, your entrapment, your diagnosis and see it through a higher, wider lens. You will see the other patterns—of family, community and culture—that are woven into your story, becoming increasingly aware of the collective story that affects everything and everyone in the world.

Sensing your part in this story, you'll feel more responsible for the choices you make, for the way you treat others—even for the thoughts you think. You'll become fascinated with your own story —and you'll begin to share it. This will help, and even guide others to examine their lives, their stories, more closely. When they do, you'll offer support and partnership. You'll give generously, from the heart, knowing that in a Divine universe, what you give is always returned to you, multiplied by Grace.

You will hurry less and put less pressure on yourself to 'win' some imaginary race to the top. Now you see that *the race* and *the top* are both illusions. You'll experience less stress at work and at home and yet, strangely, you will *have* more. Money will show up when you need it. Opportunities will materialize out of thin air.

You will begin to experience yourself as part of a flowing, living universe..

Your life, once fragmented and compartmentalized, will pull into wholeness. For your life is not just a series of unrelated events; it is one story, one gesture. You will become curious about that gesture, wondering, what is the deeper purpose for my life? What am I here to accomplish? As you ask these questions, answers will come.

This is how it is in the Sea of Miracles — a sacred story, a sacred world in which all things are sacred — including you.

Today, as I sit to write this, one image keeps returning to my mind: the vision of one person rising from a chair. I see this image again and again: one person, standing; one person, rising up. The vision arrives, as visions often do, with a download of understanding. I understand that I am being shown this vision to illustrate the wave of change, the global awakening that is sweeping the world one person, one 'rising' at a time.

The person in this vision is you. (It's also me — and everyone we know.)

You see, I believe that the angels are here for a reason: You. *You asked. You called. You want more.*

You are not alone in this. People all over the world are praying for hope, for help, for intervention; for the healing of our planet, our bodies and our broken hearts. In every language, we are calling out to every deity: *Please.*

In response, there is this rising — a rising so powerful and so huge that it is shaking our very institutions to the core — crumbling walls and even, governments. At the same time, breakthroughs in technology, medicine and science are transforming the ways in which we live, communicate and congregate. All part of the rising — the most astonishing example is our rapid evolution into a globally interconnected world.

On a more personal level, my clients tell me, "I feel so unsettled. As if there's something I'm supposed to be doing. But I can't figure out what it is?" They are having powerful dreams, they tell me. They feel as if they are swelling from the inside out, bursting with energy and an urgency they can't explain and can't understand how to use. And of course, this is what happens when we pray for change: *change comes* — but it rarely comes in the ways that we expect.

When we ask: *please guide me to health,* we are guided to: *eat healthier food, give up caffeine, and exercise.* When we pray for an end to the arguing in our marriage we find a ballerina magnet in the mud. We look outside for rescue and we are returned, endlessly, patiently to ourselves.

Which brings us to the secret that all masters know: *when we pray for change the Divine changes us.* It's the simplest truth of all, the cornerstone of all spiritual teaching: *to bring the Divine to Earth, you must bring it here yourself. To live in a Sea of Miracles, you must create it and let it shine into the world, through you.*

When you do, you will discover that the whole world is a miracle — designed to support, nourish and love you into the fullest expression of who you really are.

This love is in the rain falling from the sky, gathering into puddles and ponds—and asking nothing but that you hold out your cup. This love is in the air that you breathe, the sun that warms your skin, the food on your plate.

Are you hungry? Here's a plum, a purple valentine. You don't have to believe in God to enjoy its color, its scent and its sweetness. It's a gift—and it's all for you. This glass of water, glistening and clear; this plum with its magic seed at its center—a seed that could, if you simply planted it, yield a tree!

This is a miracle! Every time you sit down at the table. A gift: the light that illuminates this page, your incredible body with its marvelous senses; your mind with its ability to question, your heart with its wisdom and vast capacity to love.

You are a miracle—you and me, and everyone we know—and the rising energy that we feel is the answer to our prayers.

Did you get that? This rising that you feel is the answer to your prayers.

How do I know? I have lived it. I have seen it. I am a witness for the angels—and the rising of the gifts that they inspire: Peace, Wholeness, and a love so sweet and a light so bright that it burns through any darkness.

The rising in the world is wiser and wider than a faltering economy; it's a peace with roots so deep that no terrorist could ever shake them. It's the rising of a response from an interconnected All That Is which, whether you call it God, Collective Consciousness, The Universe or Baba (or any other name) is not going anywhere—a force that loves you so fully and so fiercely that it will settle for nothing less than the fullest expression of who you are.

So, what are you, really? What is this fullness that is pushing to express itself through you, through me? Nothing less than the light, love and life energy of the Divine itself!

146

So while I can't *prove* that the angels are showing up more openly and more often than ever before, I have never been more certain of anything. To me, the angels' presence is a call to action, a call that *we called* into form. I believe the angels are here to help us live in a new way — and to create a new world — *because we asked them to.*

As I finish this book, I look out into this time of terrorists, tidal waves and social upheaval and I ask for help. *How can we live without driving ourselves crazy with fear? How can we tap into the deep and ancient wisdom of the world?* I ask and I ask — and each time, I get the same answer: *Turn toward the light. Choose toward love. In this way, you will create a new pattern and the energy of the world will flow to fill it.*

I don't ask you to believe in angels. I don't need you to change anything about the way that you think or perceive the world at all. All I ask is that you take one simple step, and make this one request: Quiet your mind, take a deep breath and, with a willing and open heart, say: *Show me.*

In this way, you've invited the angels into a sacred conversation that can (and will) change your life. And that will change the world.

TWENTY-FOUR

One last story...

Last year, my husband and I drove our youngest daughter to college. Though she would be only 30 minutes away, she would no longer be a part of our daily lives—our dinner table, our morning drive to school, our shared coffee at the diner after a movie. Like her brother, she'd be moving, ever deeper into her own life, ever so steadily out of mine.

I'd been stoic as we'd packed the car and dropped her off. I hadn't made a tearful scene in the dorm room as I hugged her goodbye.

But now, as our car approached the bridge toward home, tears filled my eyes. Matthew reached over and we drove, holding hands, for a while. "I'll be able to write now," I said. "I'll be able to travel and teach."

"You will," my husband said, "and I'll have more time, too. I'll finish my book, launch my design projects."

"You will," I nodded. I pulled out a tissue, blew my nose. As we drove onto the bridge, a simple prayer filled my mind—and my heart. "Michael," I said aloud, "We are all starting something new. Please watch over Katie and Max, and over us." Matthew squeezed my hand.

The next moment, whoosh! From out of nowhere, a bright purple scarf flew up from over the side of the bridge and flapped in the wind alongside my car window. Then, it slipped back over the edge of the bridge and disappeared. Amazed, my husband and I looked at each other and we laughed.

I've got her, that purple scarf had told us. And I've got you…

∞

The angels have got you, too. I encourage you to reach out to them — today and everyday. I encourage you to find the quiet chamber of your heart and invite the Divine into conversation. I invite you to rise up and invite the Sea of Miracles to show itself to you!

As the angels showed me, *You are loved. You are precious. You are meant to be happy, fully alive and filled with peace.*

Deepening

Affirmation:
I am part of a living sea of miracles—and the Sea of Miracles is a part of me. It is an endlessly circulating living flow of giving and receiving, expanding and becoming of which I—and all that I see—are a blessed part. Life is a circle of giving and receiving. When I have abundance, it increases abundance for the world. I know that when I offer my life in service to something greater than myself I will be led to my right work, right place and right people.

Invocation:
Angels, help me to know you. Help me to use what I have learned, and all that I have gained, to heal the world. Guide me to the people who need what I have to give. Support me, at the same time, by guiding me to those who will teach me what I need in order that I may lead, teach and continue to grow.

What the angels showed me:
You are made of the same essential god-stuff as we are. At the essential level you and we and the Divine are one.

How to live a divinely-inspired life

- **Cultivate Wonder:** Be amazed and enchanted by the world around you. Actively seek out beauty. Look for things to delight you, to charm you. This opens the heart to joy.

- **Look around the room:** In this moment now, ask, What's here? What thoughts are passing through my mind that are keeping me out of the present moment? This opens the way to mindfulness—and mindfulness opens the way to presence.

- **Know yourself:** Deepen your friendship with the *I Am* that lives within your own heart. This opens the way to the soul and its purpose.

- **Develop a Mountaintop Perspective:** Seek to take a wider, wiser view of the circumstances of your life. This opens your eyes, allowing you to disconnect from pettiness and to discern and focus on what really matters to you.

- **Know your own mind:** Learn to discern which thoughts are generating from you and which are borrowed from media, from other people. This opens the way to guidance and new opportunity.

- **Know your own heart:** Choose toward love, asking continually, in all things, does this choice bring me closer to or farther from love. This opens the way to joy.

- **Share your light:** Use resonance to feel for and find what Joseph Campbell called, "your bliss." Then, follow that bliss to create the world you want to live in for there is 'art' and creativity available in all things—including your job, your home, your relationships and even, your health. This opens the way to a life of meaning, mission and purpose.

- **Ask for help:** When it comes, acknowledge it, for gratitude is the natural response to Grace. This opens the way to reverence, to humility and to the divinely given truth that you are not alone.

- **Ask the angels:** Show me the good in the world. Amplify the guidance that you send to me. Make the signs unmistakable, my intuition crystal-clear. Sharpen my ability to receive, interpret and understand the guidance you send. Open my eyes, strengthen my heart and lend me the courage to choose toward light, love and life. This opens the way to miracles.

- **Tell a new story:** Deepen your understanding of the time in which you are living—for this is not only a time of terror and peril, it is a time of rebirth and renewal. Insist on telling this story—the story that you know in your heart to be true. See your part in the glorious unfolding.

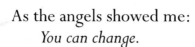

As the angels showed me:
You can change.
Imagine the world in which you want to live,
and ask for it with all your heart. Anything can heal,
anything can shift, all things are constantly changing.
All things are possible. The world is designed to call you
into engagement, and to respond to your call for support,
encouragement and peace.

Meditation:
Revealing the pattern of who you really are

We are going to make a new pattern—a new form or container into which the energy of your life can flow. Doing this is easy and no different from the process you use when daydreaming, planning a party, imagining yourself in a new outfit or situation. Yet, simple as it seems, this series of visualizations continues to be one of the most profoundly powerful, life changing exercises I've ever worked with. I offer it here as my closing gift for you.

Blessings on your beautiful life!

Note: I've recorded all of the meditations in this book. Here's the link to download to your iPod or computer: http://amyoscar.com/sea-of-miracles-meditations/.

In your mind's eye, begin to create an image of yourself as you would be if you were truly living your purpose; expressing your full, vibrant creative self, fully a part of the flow of the Sea of Miracles, fully supported by the angels.

Just make it up—if you lived in a Divine world, how would your body feel? How would you hold yourself? What would you be wearing? How would your hair be styled? What would your relationships feel like? How would you relate to your parents, your partner, your children, your friends? In a Divine world, what would your daily life be like? What kind of car would you drive? Where would you work? What would you do for a living? What would you eat for breakfast, for lunch, for dinner? Where would you eat? What kind of home would you live in? Where would it be? What would it look like, feel like? What kind of architecture? What colors? How would the rooms be furnished?

What do you want to learn, to see, to know? Where would you take your vacations? Would you tour the world, tasting new foods, trying on new clothing? Would you see ancient ruins, rainforests? Perhaps you'd swim with dolphins or watch for whales? Would you cruise to a tropical island? Would you take an eco-vacation? Would you have an RV—to drive across the country? How about a boat—a sailboat, speedboat, pleasure cruiser, yacht?

Would you help others? You don't have to—really, check in. Would you? If so, how? Would you join the Peace Corps? Would you serve soup at a homeless shelter? Would you visit senior citizens? Would you adopt or foster a child? Would you donate your time, your money, your energy? Where? Would you build houses? Rescue wildlife? Deliver medical supplies? What calls to you?

We are going to form a mental image of what you would look like, and how you would feel if you were living that life. Allow

the image to form clearly and fully. Allow yourself to see and feel the details with all of your senses.

Imagine yourself wearing those clothes, that hairstyle—living that life. See yourself engaging in those activities. Take yourself through a typical day in that dream life. Where would you have breakfast? What would you eat? Move through the day. To work, to lunch, afternoon activity, dinner. What would you do in the evening? See yourself climbing into bed at the end of a full ideal day and giving thanks for the many blessings in your life.

Give yourself all the time you need to build this image clearly and vividly in your mind's eye. If you need to, stop here and return when you're ready. When you have a clear image in your mind, continue with the next part of the exercise.

You have formed a mental image of your ideal self, living your ideal life.

Imagine her standing before you. Look into her eyes. Allow yourself to connect with her, holding her gaze and feeling her energy connect with your own.

Let her know that you are going to make a copy of her energy pattern. Feel her silently agree to let you do this. Now, watch as a glowing cloud of energy lifts from her body and stands—a glowing human outline filled with white light—between you and your ideal self. When I do this, the energy pattern looks like a glowing white cloud of high-frequency light in the shape of a human body.

Step into the pattern. Feel the light fill you—let it drench every cell of your body, your psyche, your will. Feel the life spirit pulsing through you and around you.

Feel into the pattern. This is the resonant vibration of *you* successful, *you* powerful, *you* beautiful, *you* happy. This is the vibration of your true self at its highest potential.

How does it feel? Feel around inside of the pattern. What are its qualities of energy, tone, color, density—feel into the vibration. Allow yourself to read this energy, to interpret and to know it. Allow it to teach you something about yourself.

Sit quietly inside of the pattern for at least a full minute—or longer—letting the new energy pattern penetrate.

Feel your body begin to align with this shimmering, this pattern.

Feel your energy pattern align with and begin to resonate with it.
Feel the light fill your body from your feet to the top of your head.
Feel it spreading out through the soles of your feet into the earth.
Feel it pouring out of the top of your head into the sky.
If you haven't already done so, let yourself fall in love with how this feels.
Sit inside of that love for a few moments.
Take a deep breath and say, internally or aloud, *I choose this now.*
Feel the shift.

Now, take a deep breath… and another one and open your eyes.

∞

By stepping into this pattern, your body has been programmed to resonate with it—and to recreate it. By loving this pattern—and how it feels to be inside of it—your heart has been programmed to resonate with it and to recreate it. By experiencing this pattern with your thoughts, your mind has been programmed to recreate it.

In the months to come, do this exercise as often as you like but *at least once a day* until you can call on this ideal self-image on your own. Continue to build on the image, letting it change as your aspirations evolve.

You might take a photograph of yourself and make a vision board—a collage of images cut from magazines, catalogs interspersed with photos of yourself placed in scenes where you'd like to be in real life. By activating this pattern, you have set into motion a new resonance with a new way of living.

This will naturally draw new experiences toward you. In the days and weeks to come, allow yourself to notice these new people, new opportunities—allow yourself, also, to notice new ways of thinking about yourself and the world. These new perceptions, people and experiences have been called by you and are being sent to help support your continued expansion into your new pattern. These things are responses to your call—your prayer. They are guidance.

Questions People Ask Me

ON ANGELS

"You write about *angels!?* Wow! So, what are angels, anyway?"
(Asked by an old friend at a high school reunion.)

Here's my 'cocktail party' explanation: angels are messengers—
a bridge—that allow us to communicate with God. Some angels
arise in response to our questions and prayers. They arrive (often out
of the blue) and lend a hand. Then, they recede, often disappearing without a trace. Others, like the archangels, aris from the collective—they are archetypal forms, available to all of us, all the time.

Seriously? You really believe this?

Yes. I have no doubt that there is a responsive, loving presence
guiding and helping humanity. I know how to contact it, and I know
the feeling I experience when it responds. However, I am not clair-
voyant, and I cannot yet see the angels with my eyes. To me, they
'appear' as shifts in the resonance of energy that I sense, intuitively.
To me, angels 'feel' like streams or clouds of light.

So, where are the angels, now?

Right here, all around us. You have the opportunity to work with
the angels anywhere, anytime by responding to what comes with
love. If your heart opens to someone in need, it's an invitation to
help. How will you meet this invitation, this calling? Will you keep
driving by? Or will you answer?

Can one wear out one's welcome with Archangel Michael?
Do he and the other archangels tire of the incessant appeals/
requests for help?

The short answer is no. We cannot wear out our welcome with

any of the angels; they're *angels*—timeless and also without judgment. They arise out of and respond to our call for friendship, help, reassurance—and miracles. They can be with all of us simultaneously; there's no limit to the number or the nature of allowable requests. The longer answer involves an awareness of the ways that we ourselves limit our engagement with the angels—and with other people.

Our assumption or concern that we are taking up too much of the angels' time or attention has within it two errors: The first error arises out of the idea of limited resources, or scarcity. When we feel as if we are competing for resources, we may limit our request, not wanting to take more than our fair share. Know that there is no limit to the time or attention available to you. Ask for what you really, truly want—in fact, some teachers say: *Demand* what you want with clarity, certainty and faith.

The second error arises from our own insecurity—the feeling that we are not worthy of our angels' interest and support. Nothing could be farther from the truth. The angels showed me: *We love you no matter what—we will never abandon you. Ask for the comfort, reassurance and support that you need.*

Remember: angels aren't people—and have no agenda for us. We don't have to live up to their expectations; we don't have to earn their friendship. We have it—unconditionally. Allow yourself to approach them, just as you are. Allow yourself to open to the feeling and experience of someone being there for you no matter what. That's what the word *unconditional* means, without conditions. Allow yourself to let them serve and love you—any time, in any way at all.

So, what *are* Archangels?

Archangels are unique expressions of Divine energy—each representing particular universal qualities like Beauty, Authority and Wisdom. When we pray to Archangel Michael, we are asking that his qualities of strength, protection and courage stream into our lives. When we pray to Archangel Gabriel for eloquence, ease of expression, and a sense of our true mission and purpose, we are calling on those qualities in ourselves. Archangels are one of many ordering principles, woven into the interactive energetic matrix, the structure of the human psyche and the psyche of the collective.

What constitutes a miracle?

I like Picasso's take on this, "Everything is a miracle; it's a miracle that one does not dissolve in one's bath like a lump of sugar." Essentially, a miracle is the suspension of the laws of time and space that creates an effect of healing, divine intervention or grace on our behalf. Albert Einstein said, "There are only two ways to live your life. One is as though nothing is a miracle. The other is as though everything is a miracle." I'll take the second choice.

When did you become a believer in angels?

I'm not so much a believer as a witness. I still don't believe in angels the way most people do. To me, the angels are a *response* to our collective longing for connection. To me, they're an energy bridge between God and man. That's how I can understand/conceive of an archangel being everywhere at once. They're archetypal forms, called forth by our longing—and our prayers. We do not create the angels—they are unique expressions of the Divine. However, I do believe that we can call them into form so that we can interact with them.

ON GUIDANCE

- **What message do the angels have for me?**
- **The angels don't talk with me, will you ask them this question for me?**

Each question on this list arises out of the misunderstanding that you need an intermediary—me or some other 'expert'—to approach the angels. You don't. Simply ask your question directly — you can write, speak or think it. Then, listen for a response. This initiates your own conversation with the angels, which begins wherever and whenever you are now.

How do I know if what I am feeling is really guidance? Maybe it's my imagination.

Though this can be frustrating, the truth is, it really doesn't matter whether the guidance you are receiving arises from within your heart or from the angels. In a universe where all things are connected, all guidance comes from the same source.

The voice of 'true' guidance can be discerned by asking: Does this resonate with the highest good? and opening to receive the response that comes. Ultimately, guidance that arises out of true connection with the *I Am* — the core of divinity within you — is no different than guidance that originates with the angels.

Therefore, do not dwell on where guidance comes from, nor on figuring out the particular name of a guide or angel. Instead, seek to deepen your connection. In this way, as you practice sending and receiving across the Sea of Miracles, you will come to a place where you know exactly where guidance comes from.

I have prayed and prayed for money and things are desperate over here. But nothing is happening. I feel like my angels don't love me at all.

I'm sorry you are having financial troubles. I've been there — I grew up in challenging circumstances, and raised my children from paycheck to paycheck. So I know how difficult it can be. While I can't address the specifics of your situation without talking with you, I do know this: When we ask for money, the angels don't often send cash. They send help, opportunities, gifts, chance meetings — and they send *guidance*.

Try shifting your expectation of what a response to your prayer for financial help would look like. It may come through your own intuition, as a nudge or 'inkling' that may seem completely unrelated to money. For example, you may suddenly feel the impulse to visit a store or to make a phone call. Follow these inner promptings; they may lead you to a place or a person where opportunity awaits.

Allow your problem to be solved in unexpected ways. If you need a particular object—a household appliance, a car—instead of asking for the money to purchase it, ask: *Please help me find and easily pay for (name the item)* or simply say: *I now ask that (name the item) be delivered to me, fully paid for.* If you need money to pay a bill, ask that the bill be easily, quickly paid. You won't believe what can happen.

If you are looking for a job, ask your angels to guide you to work that fulfills you, work that you enjoy and feel good about doing. Ask for opportunities to be of service to others while earning a living.

Finally, instead of asking the angels to make you rich, ask: *Please bring me work that I love, that pays a good living wage, covers all of my expenses and allows me and my family to thrive.*

ON LOVE AND RELATIONSHIPS

- **How can I attract my soul mate? Can the angels bring me someone to love?**

- **Why do some people seem to have no trouble finding partners while others, like me, find it so challenging?**

I'm going to put this right out there: I don't believe in soul mates. The angels have shown me, *You are your own soul mate—once you know and experience that, the people with whom you naturally resonate will show up.*

So, it comes down to this: some people are comfortable giving and receiving love; some people find it challenging to meet others honestly. Those people who are most challenged by relationships will be those who have the most trouble accepting people and themselves as they are. To create a loving and open relationship with another, begin by creating one with the angels. Ask them to help you see your own beauty, worthiness and unique gifts. Study your own qualities. Become a student of beauty, of love in all of its expressions—poetry, music, dance, literature, film. Don't look to or wait for another person to fill your heart—your life—with love, fill it yourself. Then, when another comes along, you will be ready. Still, remember, romantic love does not perfect or complete you—that's your job: *you are your own soul mate.*

My friend (loved one) doesn't believe in angels but I know that if she did her life would improve. How can I convince her angels are real?

You can't—and frankly, it's not your job to convince her. Each of us has our own path, our own relationship with the world in which we live and with God. If you want to inspire your friend live your life the best way you know how. If your friend or loved one is open to exploring a relationship with the angels, they will naturally be drawn to ask questions. Their questions will lead them to the teachers and truths that they need. Until then, I like what the teacher known as Abraham (working through Esther Hicks) says about this one: "You can't answer a question that hasn't been asked." In other words, follow your path and allow others to follow theirs.

ON READING ENERGY

- **You talk about reading energy. What exactly does that mean?**
- **What do you see when you read someone?**
- **How can I learn to do what you do?**

For me, story is a psychic structure, a form that exists, not in the mind but in the fields of the body, especially the heart. In a kind of intuitive 'blink,' through conversation and asking questions, a picture builds in my mind's eye. I follow clues, examining everything a client says or does — gestures, habits of speech, including, also, coincidental events that occur in the session. Everything has meaning.

As a client talks with me, I begin to perceive areas in the story that are missing or hidden. These are the places where I perceive blocked energy, suppressed experience — cars. By asking questions about the scars, I help my client to perceive them — often for the first time. Then we work together on 'homework' the client can take up toward healing.

ON HEALING

Can I send healing to someone else?

Yes, but you cannot control the outcome. Your prayers can add support to the healing process of another person — or, if it's their time to die, your prayers will help ease their transition.

Simply ask, *Please send your healing light to <name the person> for the highest good for all involved.* Then, let go of the outcome, knowing that each of us is always in God's hands.

ON ANGELS AND LAW OF ATTRACTION

Can you explain the difference between Law of Attraction and angels?

One is a law, a governing, ordering principle of creation. The other is a living presence. One dictates how things work; the other works. One is a principle of how it is; the other simply *is*. That said, I am deeply intrigued by the relationship between angels, Law of Attraction and the Divine, in general. It is at the foundation of my current research and personal exploration.

Bibliography

For an extensive bibliography of the books, workshops, and teachers who've influenced and guided my work, please visit http://amyoscar. com/love-this/

About the Author

Amy Oscar is an author, speaker and professional intuitive consultant, encouraging clients and students to develop a personal relationship with the Divine. She is the co-author (with Doreen Virtue) of My Guardian Angel: True Stories of Angelic Encounters from the readers of Woman's World magazine (Hay House, 2009). Find out more about Amy at http://www.amyoscar.com.

For more than 25 years, Amy has worked and studied with some of the most influential teachers of our time. In the 1980s, as Associate Director of Robert Fritz's New York DMA office, she helped lead teacher training workshops, and received advanced certification in Fritz's groundbreaking work with the patterning and systems of human consciousness. In the 1990s, Amy studied Biographical Counseling at Sunbridge College; in 2006, she completed a two-year training in Sacred Contracts and Spiritual Alchemy with Caroline Myss at CMED Institute. Since 2004, Amy has worked in direct collaboration with Doreen Virtue.

Acknowledgments

We are all teachers for each other, and I am deeply grateful to:

- **The thousands of people who shared a personal story of Grace** Your story inspired this book and all of my work. It was part of the sea of miracles that touched my heart more deeply than anything or anyone ever has. Now, through this book, your story will continue to resonate, touching the lives of countless others.

- **Doreen Virtue** This book would not exist without you and the radiant wisdom that your conversation with the angels has brought to me—and to the world.

- **The teachers** whose books, classes and workshops have guided me along the way with a special hug for Roger Elkrief and Chaya Spencer and a deep bow of respect and gratitude to Robert Fritz. To my 6th grade teacher, Thomas Murtphy (Great Neck JFK Elementary School), for showing me that it's okay to use colored chalk on the blackboard; and from Great Neck North High School, Carole Mitch, biology; Alphonse Liquori, History; and Marcia Levy, 11th grade English, who cried as she played us a recording of a poem. By showing me—in your playful, engaged and curious way—the thing that you loved, you changed my life.

- **Buffy,** who sees me and sits, sometimes, beaming love across a room so I can get used to living with my heart open.

- **My first editors,** Molly Thompson, Betsy Woolf, Anne Pleshette -Murphy and, with a special hug, Naomi Kenan. Thank you for giving me the break that every new writer needs.

- **S.,** who would rather not be named but to whom I am grateful.

- **My first book editor,** Lynn Wiese, who helped cut this enormous project down to size and to put things in proper order.

- **The designer of this beautiful book:** Julie Favreau Schwartz of Wyndjammr Design.

- **The brave 'first readers' who waded through my long first draft and the generous 'last readers' who volunteered to polish the final manuscript** with special mention to Pastor Allen Gibson of Memorial United Methodist Church in Elizabethtown, Kentucky; and the '9:30 North' study group.

- **My radio producer, co-host and dear friend** Janet Paist for weekly rambles and far too infrequent brunches. I am so glad the angels introduced us!

- **My guides, counselors and soul friends** Rebecca Elia, David Grady, Tom Hair, Jamie Kiffel-Alcheh, Michael Melia, Catherine Parker, Susan Powers, Suzanne Saltzman, Taryn Phillips-Quinn, Suzanne Weiss.

- **My 'girls,'** who grew up with me and who, therefore, know exactly who I am: Hilarie Kurien, Gayle Ulmann, Susan Walsdorf, Freddi Weiss.

- **Julia Parzen,** who raised my children with me, and who holds her end of the string of our friendship so that, each time I pick up my end, she is there. (I love you.)

- **My father,** who taught me to walk in my own way, to laugh at the great absurdity, to ask questions and especially, lately, showed me what true courage looks like.

- **My mother,** who read to me. My mother, who painted me in bold colors when I was 12, arms open wide, with wings of white light. My children's grandmother. My mother, who loves.

- **Esther,** who teaches me (daily) what devotion looks like.

- **My sisters, Beth and Jen,** blessed companions, mirrors along this wacko trail (and you know what I mean.) Friends and constant teachers, your humor, courage and wisdom amaze and inspire me. PS Thank you for loving my children and for teaching them to laugh.

- **Max,** my first true love, who shows me, every day, what steady daily practice means and who talks with me about life and shadow and the simple gifts of tomato soup.

- **Katie,** who sees the world of patterns and mirrors that I see; and who teaches me, because she is better at it, how to navigate that world.

- **My husband, Matthew,** mate of my heart, soil in which I'm planted, foundation upon which I'm built — my world.

- **The angels** who need no words to know.

My life has been blessed beyond words by each of you.

Amy Oscar
July 2011
2nd Edition

Share your story!

You've heard my story — I'd love to hear yours. You can share it on my website at: http://amyoscar.com/share-your-angel-divine-story/ or by email, to amy@amyoscar.com.

To **read more Angel Stories,** sent in by the readers of my blog: http://amyoscar.com.

To preview my next book: **Sea of Miracles: The Stories,** http://amyoscar.com/stories-from-the-sea-of-miracles/.

To preview Shadow and Light, my beautiful card set with lush seasonal imagery from Susan Powers, and inspiring words from me: http://amyoscar.com/shadow-and-light/.